A YANKEE IN MENORCA

Lana Johnson

Raider Publishing International

New York   London   Cape Town

First Printing

The views, content and descriptions in this book do not represent the views of Raider Publishing International. Some of the content may be offensive to some readers and they are to be advised. Objections to the content in this book should be directed towards the author and owner of the intellectual property rights as registered with their local government.

All characters portrayed in this book are fictitious and any resemblance to persons living or dead is purely coincidental.

ISBN: 978-1-61667-320-8

Published By Raider Publishing International
www.RaiderPublishing.com
New York London Cape Town
Printed in the United States of America and the United Kingdom

For Paula, the reason I finally believe in myself. Thank you. And for Nicolas, who has made my experiences in Menorca so truly Menorquín

Acknowledgements

My deepest thanks to Paula who encouraged this project, read every chapter as it was written, gave invaluable insight and suggestions, designed the cover, spurred me on and made so much of this story in itself happen. Paula, you are an amazing friend and person.

Huge thanks to my Mom who has always believed in me and made me feel that I could do anything. Thank you for not making me feel guilty about living so far away and for supporting me no matter what.

Thank you to my Auntie Anne who has always been a constant in my life. Thank you for teaching me the importance of keeping stories alive and for telling me so many stories of the quirky and amazing women in our family. I wish you would write a book.   Many   thanks to Carisa who has helped me since childhood to dream up crazy ideas like going to live in a foreign land. Thank you for cherishing our friendship enough to not let an ocean between us hinder our closeness.

And of course, thank you Menorca and all of its wonderful people that have accepted me and made my life such an interesting adventure.

A YANKEE IN MENORCA

Lana Johnson

Contents

"The Balearic Islands are like women. Ibiza is the woman who will destroy you. Mallorca is the woman who will always be out of your reach. And Menorca is the woman you will always want to go back to."

An old fisherman's comment when I told him I had not visited the other islands.

"If the Mediterranean was a book, Menorca would be a beautiful poem read out in a whisper."

Unknown, but obviously someone who has been here and stayed a while.

1

Mushrooms?

Anxiety tinged with excitement gnawed at me throughout the day. Fierce emotions took turns possessing me, causing hand wringing and tears one moment and giggles of optimism at the thought of a shinny, happy and adventurous future the next. In the last week, I had graduated from college, packed my bags, boarded a flight and said goodbye to the country I had lived in for twenty-three years.

I tried to keep my nervousness at bay by telling myself that at least I spoke the language of the country I would now call home, Spain. I imagined and even practiced witty remarks I would make at parties, dazzling new friends with my Spanish proficiency.

I knew that, in Menorca, they spoke Menorquín, a dialect of Catalan. Many people tried to reassure me that Catalan was only a dialect of Spanish, which I surely could pick up within a few months. I knew this was not the case and that Catalan was as different from Spanish as is any other romance language. However, Fernando, my new husband, promised me that every person who spoke Catalan, and any dialect of it, also spoke Spanish.

Knowing this, I again controlled my rising apprehension with the comforting thought that all of my years of studying Spanish would now pay off. Within the first week on new soil, I realized how wrong I was.

*   *   *   *

In California, Central and South American Spanish grammar and vocabulary are typically taught. I even remember, when learning how to conjugate verbs in high school, my Spanish professor said, "The conjugation '*vosotros*' is only used in Spain, so we will not waste our time learning it; just keep in mind it exists."

After six years, I still cannot successfully use this conjugation, often leading my friends and loved ones to think I am talking about others instead of to them.

The difference was shocking and angering at first. I had studied so hard only to find out that about a third of what I had learned was irrelevant in my new home. I was constantly irritated that people could not understand me when I was speaking clear and precise Spanish. After many frustrated tears and bad thoughts aimed at Spaniards, I accepted that being irritated with others was not the solution and started learning Spanish again.

It took me a long time to feel comfortable using the verb '*coger*', which, in Spain, is probably the most commonly used verb, meaning to take, hold, grab, and get, but everywhere else it is the most vulgar term for sexual relations. Unfortunately, I had just become comfortable with the word before visiting Argentina and asked to *coger* everything from newborns to kayaks.

In many situations, I was not understood, but I would explain what I wanted and then learned the word used here. Some words were easier to mime than others, but I never seemed to be hung up on a word for too long despite the fact that Menorcan people seem to be the worst charade players in the world. That or they just enjoy me making an ass out of myself.

One of these bad-charades-player/me-making-an-ass-out-of-myself situations happened when I first arrived and noticed that almost all of the women on the island had wicker baskets they used for grocery shopping. It seemed very logical because everyone walks to the bread store, *panadería*, then to the butcher shop, *carnicería*, then to the fruit and veggie stand, *verdulería*, and then to the supermarket for whatever else. Apart from the convenience of carrying all of these little purchases around comfortably, I also just liked how a fresh baguette of bread looked sticking out of these baskets. It looked so Mediterranean. I had to have one, feeling sure that this would make me more of a Menorcan woman. I asked a woman on the way to the *verdulería* with her basket where I could purchase one. She looked at me strangely and asked, "What is it you want to buy?"

"*Una canasta,*" I said, repeating the word for basket.

She continued to look at me like I was very weird, so I pointed at her basket. She pulled out a baguette of bread and started giving me directions to the *panadería*. After a few more tries of pointing at her basket and getting more items pulled out, she finally understood and told me that the word in Spain for this type of basket was *cesta*. I gave the woman a three on a scale of one to ten for her charades ability, but I do now have a very nice *cesta* with strong leather straps.

I began to notice that my vocabulary and way of speaking were changing little by little. I started saying *dígame* or just *hola* when answering the phone instead of saying *bueno* like I had learned in Mexico. I was now ordering *zumo* instead of *jugo* when I wanted juice, saying *aquí* instead of *acá* for here, and was now *coger*-ing everything without blushing. But, apart from these little things, I had never had a *major* problem understanding or being understood here until I came down with a sinus infection.

I hate taking antibiotics, scared that my body will become accustomed to them and they will no longer work when they really need to. But I was tired of holding my towel-covered head over a pot full of steaming water, which I had tried for two weeks to no avail, and I could stand the pressure in my cheekbones no longer.

The antibiotics, which I amazingly received from the pharmacy without a prescription, worked their magic, killing everything good and bad in my body and leaving me with a feminine itch I had been dreading since I started them. In the United States, these kinds of situations do not present a problem. You can go down to the nearest convenience store and pick the appropriate medication off the shelf, and there you go, problem solved. However, in Spain, you have to go to the pharmacy and ask for everything from over the counter pain relievers to toothpaste to beauty products.

I did not know the word for yeast infection (not something you learn in school), so I explained my symptoms to my husband. He said, "*Hongos...* You have *hongos.*"

I stared at him aghast, and then hotly told him that I did not have *hongos!* I had learned that word very well in Mexico, mushrooms...the kind you eat. I love mushrooms and, therefore, was sure of the word. I learned the word from my text book in the chapter dealing with the vocabulary of fruits and vegetables. So, when I heard the word *hongos*, the image of a perfect mushroom that I would put on a salad or pizza popped into my head. Definitely not what I had.

"I don't want the slang, gross word for what I have. I want the technical term so I can go down and tell the pharmacist as quickly as possible what I have without having to go into detail."

Fernando rolled his eyes and repeated my mushroom diagnose.

"I want a euphemism for what I have. I am not going down to tell the pharmacist that I have mushrooms in my private parts; God knows what he will give me to cure that."

"If you do not believe me, go down to the pharmacy and ask."

There was no way I was going to do that, so I kept at it. "What is it that makes bread rise?"

"Lana, bread is not going to help you in this situation."

Men! However, his asinine comment and the image it conjured up made me remember something about yogurt. Something about the cultures in natural yogurt was about to surface. Was it for yeast infections? Or was it another type of infection? Or was it good for the complexion? Crap.

"Just listen, what is the bacteria that they put in bread to make it rise?"

"They put bacteria in bread in the USA?"

Men!

"Just tell me what the hell you put in bread to make it rise!"

"*Levadura* I think."

I seem to have a natural feel for knowing if a word in another language presented to me is the correct one, and felt this was not right. I looked up 'yeast' in my Spanish to English dictionary and the word was, indeed, *levadura*. However, I still did not feel the word was the one I was looking for at the particular moment. Maybe the word the Spanish use had nothing to do with the name of the actual bacteria.

I realized that I had run out of immediate options, so, reluctantly, I walked to the pharmacy. To my relief, there was no one else and the female assistant, Carmen, was there and appeared to be alone. The pharmacy is the hub of gossip in Es Migjorn Gran and Carmen is the queen bee gossip. She knows everything about everyone and not just medically related facts. Therefore, I was not going to tell her that my husband told me to come here and tell her I had mushrooms *down there*. I could just see all the people of Es Migjorn Gran having a good laugh at the only Yankee in town going to the pharmacy and declaring that she had mushrooms in her *chocho*. I did not trust my husband on this one. So I explained my symptoms and, to my dismay, she said, "You have *hongos*."

"No," I screeched. I took a deep breath. "*Infección de levadura?*"

"*Qué?*" The completely-at-a-loss look on Carmen's face confirmed that I was right when I felt the word was not the one I was looking for.

Then, to my horror, I heard, "*Hongos*; you have *hongos*," from the back as the male pharmacist walked around the corner.

I am not a shy person, but I did not want the male pharmacist who goes sailing with my husband and whom I pass daily to tell me I had mushrooms in my private parts.

"Is there no better way to say it?" I croaked. "No euphemism?"

"Nope, mushrooms are mushrooms and that's what you've got," replied the ever-helpful Carmen.

Other people had walked into the pharmacy by this time and I felt the blood rush to my face and big red blotches appear on my chest. Even my ass was sweating with embarrassment. So yes, it was now confirmed, the red-faced, blotchy chest Yankee had *hongos* in her *chocho*.

They gave me my mushroom cure and I went red faced back to my house. My husband could have been gracious, but instead he asked as I closed the door, "So, did they tell you that you have *hongos?*"

Without replying, I went in to my room, slammed the door and called my mom to tell her about this most unfortunate translation.

I now know that *champiñones* or *setas* are the general words for mushrooms (the kind you eat) in Spain.

2

Cavalleria

'There are places like Cavalleria that take on the aspect of the end of the world, of a truly supernatural landscape', Carlos Garrido wrote in his book, *Menorca Mágica,* and it is true. I look at the Cape of Cavalleria, the northernmost tip of Menorca, every day from a window of the farmhouse Santa Teresa and still get goose-bumps. The tip of the cape is covered in little piles of stones, stacked one on top of another, thousands of them. People feel the need to mark that they have been there and left something... maybe in exchange for sharing its beauty.

The cape dips down to sea level, granting access to the small, white-sand cove of Cala Viola, or known to many as 'goat beach'. Every morning, the farmer comes in his feeding truck, honking his horn, while all the goats in the cape come running to Cala Viola, which has been their feeding place since birth. After the cape's dip into the sea, it rises to meet the sky, crowned by the oldest lighthouse on Menorca. It then drops off abruptly into unforgiving rock cliffs that, coupled with the strong *tramontana* winds, gave the area its nickname, the Anti-Christ Coast, by sailors through time because of its danger and claim to passing ships. The cliffs of the Cape of Cavalleria shape the profile of a woman's face. She is Cavalleria and looks out over the

Mediterranean and the graveyard of ships that have broken against her chin and now lie beneath her lips.

The natural port of Sanitja sneaks by her gaze to the left, snaking in among the shrubs and red dirt. It has been a refuge since ancient times for sailors attempting the Anti-Christ Coast. Through the *Posidonia*, the protected Neptune Grass that grows on the bottom of the port, shards of roman pottery, ship timbers and more modern hulls can be seen. Not all ships find safe harbor here.

You can feel the energy rising off the rocks baking in the sun and the determination of the rugged vegetation that endure the punishing winds and salt. Many people have told me something like, "I don't really believe in all of that energy stuff, but I have to admit that this place has energy... I can feel it." And you can. I always reply that surely this is why so many different cultures have inhabited this place. The *Talayotic* culture had a settlement nearby, the Romans were here for around 600 years, then there was a Muslim occupation, followed by the British and finally by the current inhabitants, the Olivars, a family of noble decent that was given the land by the King of Spain.

It is true that many sites have been used by various cultures, sites of worship, for example. Build the cathedral on top of the Pagan temple so it will be easier to convert the indigenous people. However, this is not what happened in Cavalleria. Each new occupant of the area arrived after the previous culture had left. It was not that they came because there were already people established; therefore, making it easier. No, it was as if each culture was independently drawn here.

People often are confused as to what to call the place because there are so many names used by locals when referring to the area: Cavalleria, the name of the northernmost cape. Santa Teresa, the name of the farmhouse and surrounding farm. Sanitja, the natural port that grazes along the left of the cape. Sanisera, the Roman city that occupied the cape. Ecomuseum, the museum that explains about the cultural and natural heritage of the area, which is located in the northern half of the farmhouse Santa Teresa. All of these names refer to the northernmost tip of the island. If a local says 'Cavalleria', it most often means the beach of Cavalleria. 'Santa Teresa' usually translates to hunting in the area, which requires permission of the farm owners. People who lived in Santa Teresa, working for the noble family, also refer to the entire area by this name. 'Sanitja' means fishing in the port. I would like to think only fishing from the rocks with a pole, which is legal in this natural reserve. However, it is much more likely to mean illegally fishing with a spear gun. 'Sanisera' means visiting the ruins, hopefully without a metal detector. 'Ecomuseum' translates to having a drink on the terrace that provides the best view of the Mediterranean.

*   *   *   *

When explaining the history of Menorca to a friend, he said, "Menorca sounds like the whore of the Mediterranean. Everyone has been here and had their way with her."

The Romans were the first to arrive here in 123 BC. They established a small military fort. From what Fernando has unearthed in his excavations, the camp was small and not overly fortified. Due to the large amount of rounded sea stones, lead projectiles and lead slag left over from smelting them found in the Roman camp along with *Talayotic* pottery, it seems that the camp was more of a recruiting area for the famous Balearic Slingshot Warriors who worked as mercenaries in the Roman army. I was, at first, unimpressed with the idea of a sling slinging rounded stones and lead projectiles at enemies until Fernando told me that a lead projectile of a Balearic Slingshot Warrior could travel further and with more accuracy than an arrow shot from a bow by an archer. "This is why the Romans used the Balearic Slingshot Warriors in the first part of an attack. There is great example of this in a battle scene of the movie *Alexander the Great*," Fernando, ever the professor, told me, and I remembered the scene, gaining a much greater respect for the weaponry used by the indigenous culture of the Balearics.

After fifty years, the Romans decided to abandon the fort and move to the other side of the port of Sanitja, where they founded the city of Sanisera. For 600 years, the city flourished due to the maritime commerce receiving ships going from Spain to Italy and from France to Africa.

I always wondered how people knew these kinds of things; the name of the ancient cities, maritime trade routes, what ships stopped from where, what their cargo was, how long certain cultures occupied certain territories, etc. I was pleased to find out that I was not the only one when Fernando asked me to translate an introduction of the archaeological site for a new group of archaeology students participating in the field school. The official translator was home, sick with the flu.

"Many of you may wonder how we know that this is the city of Sanisera. There are no modern publications of the site telling us. So how do we know?"

Twenty blank faces stared back at him (twenty-one, counting myself, the translator), hoping it was a rhetorical question and that he was not going to call on anyone.

"Classical sources and ancient maps are how we know the name and location of the city." He went on to explain the different sources that cited this site, like Pliny the Elder, and the ancient maps that marked the city along the ancient maritime trade routes. "Menorca is smack in the center of the western Mediterranean Sea, making it a great stopping point for those sailing the Mediterranean. So how do we know where the ships came from and what their cargo was?"

A student ventured, "Ship wrecks along the coast?"

"That's one way, but there is another way that gives us more consistent information." Fernando bent down and picked up something off the ground. "What is this?"

Various students blurted out the obvious, "Pottery."

"No, no. This, my friends, is not just pottery… This is our key to the past!"

God, I remembered now why I hate translating for Fernando. His flair for dramatics and *unique* jokes are hard to pull off in a different language and, if I failed to put the same enthusiasm into my sentences that he did, I would be in trouble later. I originally stopped translating for Fernando because he says I filter, which, of course, I deny, but, of course, I do. Spaniards do not seem to be overly concerned with being politically correct, and, being that the majority of the participants of our archaeology field school are from very politically correct countries, there is a need for a politically correct filter.

"With just this piece of pottery," Fernando continued, "I can tell you what kind of container it was, what the container carried, the time period and where it came from."

A student snorted air though his nostrils, conveying his doubts.

Fernando smiled. "The thickness of the walls of this piece of pottery tells us that it is an amphora. For those of you who do not know what that is, it was what the Romans used to transport mainly wine, cereals, olive oil, and fish sauce preserve around the Roman Empire. Amphorae to Romans are what Tupperware is to us. Pottery that has thinner walls is major common ware, for example: plates, cups, pots, etc. The thickness of this piece tells us it is an amphora, which is the majority of the type of pottery we will be finding. The most important parts of an amphora, archaeologically speaking, are the handles, bases and rims. We are especially lucky because this piece of pottery is part of the rim. From the shape of the rim, I know that this amphora carried wine. Amphorae came in many shapes and sizes, but it is usually relatively easy to distinguish certain types of amphorae from others. For example, amphorae that contained olive oil are often very small on the top, with little handles and have very large, round bottoms." He shot me a mischievous look and added in English, "Like Lana."

Luckily, all of the students laughed at his joke. Similar situations had included filtering.

"Amphorae have been studied intensively and have been inventoried and cataloged. Studying the different catalogs and comparing them to the pottery on our site, we can get a better idea of what we are working with. Roman pottery had different trends and fashions just like we have nowadays. Some types of pottery were in production for 300 years, but others only for fifty. Also, the lack of a certain type of pottery can be just as indicative as the pottery found on a given site. For example, there was a major trend in Roman pottery, which is called *Terra Sigillata*, or more commonly known as Samian ware. It was extremely popular and exported all over the Roman Empire. It began production in the last part of the first century BC. It is common ware pottery with a lush red varnish on the outside. We have found many pieces in the Roman city of Sanisera; however, we have almost finished the excavation of the Roman military fort without finding a single piece. We know from classical sources that the military fort was established in 123 BC. From the lack of *Terra Sigillata*, we know that it was abandoned before it started production and exportation in the last part of the first century BC." Fernando looked down at the piece of pottery in his hand, and said, "I know from looking at many books of pottery that this type of amphora carrying wine was made in the first century BC. Now who can tell me how I know where it is from?"

No one made a speculation and Fernando happily announced, "Little black dots. Clay by itself cannot go in a kiln at high temperatures because it would crack or break. Something needs to be mixed with it to fortify the clay. This is usually some sort of local mineral. We can identify amphorae from Tarragona, in the west of Spain, by its clearish white quartz mixed in with the clay. Here we have a moderately heavy, reddish-orange clay with little black dots. Any guesses as to what and where?"

No one guessed and Fernando added, "Think Pompeii."

Half blurted out 'lava' while the others said 'Italy', answering both parts to Fernando's last question.

Fernando looked at his new students approvingly and said, "Yes, in parts of Italy where there was volcanic activity, they mixed their clay with bits of lava. From this little piece of pottery, we know that it was an amphora carrying wine produced in the first century BC from Italy. Not bad. As we go down layer by layer, the pottery will tell us the chronology of the site. Archaeological artifacts are not all that informative in isolation; it is the context that they are found in that tells us history. This is why looting of archaeological sites is such a horrendous act... It destroys the context and erases history."

The students ate up his words and I could see a new group of cultural heritage defenders forming.

*   *   *   *

I had heard the term 'Moors' in history class and remembered for the exam that their departure from Spain was when Columbus sailed the ocean blue, but knew little more of their Spanish occupation. When I arrived, I heard the word *moros* often when referring to people from North Africa. I assumed it must mean Moors, which I assumed must be the term for people from North Africa (I wish I would have remembered my mother's saying, 'to assume makes an ass out of you and me'). I noticed strange looks when I told Spanish tourist about the '*moros*' of Cavalleria, but did not know why until Fernando overhead me and explained.

"Lana, *moros* is now a very derogative and offensive term that only people considered racist use."

Perfect, I thought. The only politically incorrect word in Spain and I had been using it daily. Sexual innuendos, sexual harassment, discriminatory references (apart from *moro*)... not a big deal. But I had been freely shouting the one 'no-no' word in Spain. Fantastic. I know now to say Muslim occupation and not Moorish occupation when speaking Spanish.

A small mosque, some fragments of pottery and a few silver coins are the only evidence of the Muslim occupation in Cavalleria that followed the Roman's 600-year stay in the area. Fernando had made the discovery of their occupation in the north, making my cheeks burn even more knowing now what I had told tourist. The main part of the Roman city was the only part known before he began in the area, a sole Menorcan archaeologist being the 'devirginizer' of the site, followed by Fernando. She mistakenly identified the mosque as a Roman lighthouse. Her mistake was quite understandable. The stones that were used in setting the base of the mosque had *opus caementicium* or Roman cement covering many parts of them. However, the cement did not join any two stones together.

Up until very recently on Menorca, it was common of farmers to take the larger, well-cut stones from *old walls* for more modern purposes. It looks as if this is what the

Muslim population in Cavalleria did when building their mosque. Why go through the extra work of cutting stone if you already have perfectly cut stones in that abandoned building over there?

After comparing many examples of mosques in other areas, it turned out that the fact that the *tower* of the Roman *lighthouse* faced Mecca was no coincidence.

*   *   *   *

Fishermen were the next occupants of the area. S'Almadrava, a small, whitewashed building resembling a small house on the coast of the port of Sanitja, is their mark upon the cape. It was built in the 1700s by fishermen after tuna. They hired experts from Sardinia, but had little luck in their fishing company aspirations. But their time in Cavalleria was not completely in vain because this little whitewashed structure is still used today as a common area by fishermen of Fornells and Es Mercadal[1] as a refuge and

---

[1] Technically, Fornells is part of the town of Es Mercadal, which is located in the very center of the island. Fornells is located on the coast, six kilometers to the north. At one point, Es Migjorn Gran was also part of Es Mercadal. Es Migjorn Gran (located six kilometers to the south of Es Mercadal) petitioned independence when they had established all the necessary requirements for 'townness' and it was granted. I think it would surprise anyone who has been in Fornells that it is not considered a town. They have been fighting passionately for their independence for years and, in 2007, the issue was finally taken to court and Fornells was denied independence from Es Mercadal. Everyone was shocked. This was not the outcome anyone had expected. Es Mercadal was quite pleased with the outcome as they did not lose this very beautiful, touristy and money making *urbanization* from their limits. However, the people of Fornells were crushed. Even if the courts did not, I always try to make a point of referring to them as distinctly separate places. Anyone visiting Fornells would also be wise to do this.

place to keep their fishing gear. It has a large, covered terrace that has provided us a place to have many late night, candlelit dinners of *paella* or charbroiled meat and veggies accompanied by an abundance of red wine and cynical humor brought on by a hard day of work in the north.

* * * *

The British definitely know how to make their mark on a new land. Over 300 years after their first occupation of Menorca, and people here still drink gin, eat *Mahónnaise* and use many English words that snuck their way into the Menorcan dialect.

The British introduced gin to the island during their occupation throughout the 18th century. There are few places that still produce it in the traditional way, the most popular being Xoriguer. It is heated in copper pots by a wood fire. The distillation of the juniper berries does not follow the typical British recipe to the letter and it has its own very unique Menorcan gin taste.

Mahónnaise also came from the island. I have heard many different stories about how it came to be. Some say that the French, during their short stay on the island, fell in love with a local recipe called *allioli*, which is made out of egg, olive oil and garlic. Others say that a British general who lived in Mahón (the largest town on the island) used an egg and olive oil sauce to put on his fish. He invited a French general over for dinner and the Frenchman fell in love with the sauce, took the idea back to his country and made it famous. Regardless of which story is true, one thing is clear… mayonnaise is from Menorca, not France!

Menorquín, the local dialect of the Catalan language, is chocked full of English words, even though they are almost indiscernible through the thick island accent. Menorquín, to me, sounds like Catalan underwater, as do any of the English words thrown in there.

However, when I think of the British occupation on the island, I think of the chain of defense towers along the coast. Cavalleria's panorama would not be the same if it was not for the crumbling British defense tower to the left of the port that now serves as a pedestal to the many cormorants that sun themselves like eager flashers between their dives in the port of Sanitja.

There are eleven defense towers on the island and each one has a line of sight with one other. Our defense tower has a line of sight with the one in neighboring Fornells. I was told that, in the event of an attempted invasion, the nearest tower would communicate this danger to the other tower within its line of sight via smoke so that the other vulnerable parts of the island where ships could penetrate would have ample time to prepare for the invasion. The first thing I thought of after hearing this was *Lord of the Rings* (what does that say about me?). I doubt the efficiency of this strategy because, two years after its completion in 1800, the British lost their control of the island to the Spanish.

*   *   *   *

With sailors giving the name Anti-Christ Coast to Cavalleria, it is easy to imagine why the Cape of Cavalleria lighthouse was the first on the island. The lighthouse began construction 1854 and was finished in 1857. There is a quarry next to the lighthouse, which is where its sandstone bricks came from. The rest of the construction materials were brought by boat to Cala Viola (goat beach) and then carried by mule up to the tip of the cape. A stone road was laid to make the trip easier and parts of this road can still be seen today.

The lighthouse of Cavalleria is by far the most visited place in Menorca. It is strange that this is so because it is not advertised anywhere like many of the *Talayotic* sights. I guess it is the same for everyone as it is for me; when you have a map of Menorca in your hands, you are unconscionably pulled to the north. Cavalleria calls you.

Near the tip of the cape, the landscape changes drastically. You are on the moon looking out over an azure sea. The most stunning sunset of Menorca is seen from the lighthouse of Cavalleria. As the sun tires, she slides down next to the British defense tower, saying goodnight to the content birds atop it, and then past the Roman Necropolis, with tombs orientated east to west symbolizing the begin and end in her honor. She gently warms the heads of these dead before she sinks into the sea, the colors of the day following her one by one until only black is left.

* * * *

The Olivar family was lucky enough to be there and to be noble when Spanish kings still gave out enormous expansions of land to noblemen. They were given various parts of Menorca, one of them being the northernmost part of the island now known as the Cape of Cavalleria. In the 1800s, the Olivars built the farmhouse named Santa Teresa. Looking at it today, it looks as if it was built backwards. The great arching front faces the fields, while the livestock and servants' quarters face the sea. However, I know it was built correctly because I have taken shelter on the front porch during a major storm when I forgot the keys to the museum and had to wait for the storm to let up a bit before attempting the drive back. The wind blew so hard that the entire northern surface of the house was covered in a layer of salt and one of the windows shattered inwards, not able to withstand the strength of the wind. The ground was littered with fallen roof tiles that would need to be replaced after the storm. While, on the other side, it was completely calm and difficult for me to believe that such a raging storm was in progress. Santa Teresa was built practically.

In front of the great arched entrance is a stone walkway to a small church. I was told that there was always a priest living at Santa Teresa to provide services for those who lived there, so far away from any town. In the center on a small altar is Santa Teresa (Saint Teresa). To the left of the main doors is a smaller one. Past this small green door is an old oven in the wall for baking bread.

The noble family had servants living there year round. The farmers' sons helped in the field and the wives and daughters worked in the house. Additions to the house were made when needed.[2] The Olivars usually came during summer to enjoy the small private beach behind the house and to hunt. But, for the rest of the year, it was just the servants and farmers trying to make a living off the salty, stony land.

People were born in Santa Teresa and people died in Santa Teresa. I don't believe in ghosts, but they scare me all the same and I will not stay in Santa Teresa past dark by myself.

One typical summer day, a family came to the museum accompanying an old woman. Her eyes were lucid and they danced with pleasure at everything they saw. She told me, "I was born here in Santa Teresa and my mama died here. I am eighty-eight years old, and I just wanted to see this place one more time before I die."

---

[2] There are still no plans of the house. An architect came out once and almost broke down in tears when I repeatedly opened doors that led to large uneven rooms, or pointless hallways that had doors on both ends. "This house never ends and it makes no sense!" he exclaimed.

Even though she shuffled a bit, I knew that this woman was not going to die soon despite what she said. She had a certain spark to her that many at twenty no longer have. I told her that I would be happy to show her and her family around. She stopped me before we went in and asked her family if they knew why all of the roof tiles on the outer edge were laid horizontally with the edges curving up towards the sky. With this question, I knew that her family had not been raised on Menorca as she had been, because, if they had, there would be no need for the question. "Because there is no water. The roof of Santa Teresa is designed to catch all of the rain water."

She traced the outer line of the roof tiles to where they met with a whitewashed, box-like structure that then turned into a pipe and disappeared into the house.

"There is no ground under Santa Teresa, only huge cisterns to hold the rain water."

We walked into the house and I pointed to the two indoor openings of the cistern. I explained that we now had a motor to bring the water up out of the cistern.

"Oh, but surely you do not have enough water to run this museum... How many people use the bathroom a day? We had to ration water like crazy even using an outhouse with no water and still it was not enough and we were only a few families."

I smiled at her insight and told her that we cheat. About once a month, a truck full of water comes and shoves a huge hose in the cistern opening and fills it up. She laughed and said, "Oh, if only we would have had such luxuries."

We walked past the cisterns and started up the stairs. As we climbed the stairs, she explained to me that her mom was a cook in the house and that she and her sister helped with all of the cleaning and washing.

When we reached the top of the stairs, she said without out a doubt, "This window is much bigger than what it was."

It, indeed, was, but I did not elaborate because Fernando had done this little bit of work without getting the necessary building permit, saying, 'no one can catch me because there are no plans of the house and not even the Olivars would know because this side was where the servants lived'.

"Much, much bigger," she continued. "I know because every time my papa would get on his horse to go for supplies in town, I just knew he wasn't going to come back. I stayed with my face pressed to the window all day long. Mama let me because she knew from experience that, if she tried to make me work while I was so worried, I would end up causing more work than getting it done. So I would stay with my face pressed against the small pane of glass until I saw him on his horse pulling a buggy full of supplies in the distance. I would run down the stairs, out of the yard and up the dirt road to where he was and hug him frantically while I cried. He never understood my fear. Neither did I, really, because he always came back."

We walked out onto the second-storey terrace.

"When it was really hot, we would sleep in hammocks on this terrace. My mama used to get so mad because one of the hammocks hung right next to that arch," she said, pointing to the one on the right. "When she wasn't looking, we would take turns pushing each other in the hammock through the arch and out over the wall. It was so exciting. Looking back, I can't believe we did it. If we had fallen out or the hammock broke, we could have died. God, kids are crazy. I am so glad mine are all grown," she said, looking adoringly at who I now knew was her son.

We walked back inside and she turned right while I closed the terrace doors. She had entered one of the rooms used for storage. It had a steeply angled roof with only two small ventilation windows at the top. I saw no other use for it apart from storage... but this woman helped to stretch my imagination.

"We used to fill this room with branches." That was not what I was expecting and hoped that she would clarify. "Us kids would go out and collect *caracoles* (land snails) during the good weather and put them in here with the branches that they ate. We kept this room stocked full of fresh branches and snails. By doing this, we could eat *caracoles* all winter long, not just in spring and summer."

She asked if she could see the rest of the house. We only had half of it rented out, the half where the livestock and servants quarters were, fixed up into a small museum... but a house like Santa Teresa has many tricks and I knew how to get into the other side. The other side was still occasionally used by the Olivar family on Sunday get-togethers, but there were no longer servants living there and the Olivars had not been in years. I really saw no harm, so I agreed.

We went back down the stairs and crossed the bar, and I opened a door that had a pointless and short hallway with another door at the other end. We use this double-door room as a place to keep the garbage of the day, which I have to haul in my car every day, twelve kilometers to Es Mercadal. What really angers me about this is we have to pay the same garbage taxes as the people who have bins next to their houses.

I pulled out the few bags of garbage that had accumulated from the bar that morning, grabbed a butter knife and motioned for her and family members to follow. I stuck the knife through a crack in the wood and lifted upwards, knowing that the lock was just a strip of metal painted green that lay in a J-like catch. I gave the door a push and it swung inwards. It was like walking back through time. I heard the woman suck in a deep breath and exclaim, "It is just like it was."

I am not sure exactly when the Olivar family stopped having servants in Santa Teresa, but, from the yellow and brittle newspapers on the shelf, I imagine it was a long time ago. The last *payés* of Santa Teresa lived in Es Migjorn Gran and drove every day to take care of the farm, and hardly ever went into the house. He was still the farmer of Santa Teresa while we were snooping around. After he retired, the *payés* of all Cavalleria absorbed Santa Teresa into his work load.

"Look, look, there is still the fish mounted on the wall and the stuffed partridge on the little table in the corner. My mama always griped that it was not normal to have dead things in a house out like decorations." She continued roaming around the house, lost in her nostalgia.

We all just stood back and watched.

"This is the table that the nobles used. Mama would never let us near it…. not even when they were gone. I remember once in winter I told my mama that it was not fair that they had such a nice table and hardly ever used it. I asked if we could eat there sometimes. She smacked me on the behind and told me no, because it would be disrespectful. But I think that she must have had similar thoughts because her smack was halfhearted."

We walked out the front doors. I was making a mental list of everything that I had to close up after and praying that Biel, the *payés*, would not come right then with the house doors wide open.

She walked almost trance-like to the little church and opened the doors. "This is where I went to church my entire childhood. When I was little and daydreamed about getting married, it was always in front of this little church." She turned and looked down the dirt road that passed the cow troughs carved out of *mares,* the local sandstone, then onto the fields and sea. "Is the small beach still there?"

I nodded, letting her know that it was.

"I learned to swim there," she said proudly.

We walked around in the yard and she pointed out a sun dial on the front of the house that I had never noticed. She laughed when she saw the *mares* sarcophagus and I thought maybe she was not so lucid after all. But she quelled my doubts when she began to explain. "Señor Olivar was obsessed with two things: archaeology and hunting. When we heard that he found a sarcophagus on the other side of the port and wanted to bring it here, we all thought he was crazy. We made bets as to whether or not it would break on the way over. It made it intact. None of us knew what he had done with the bones, and Mama said it was wrong to disturb the dead. I had nightmares of an angry Roman skeleton coming to get me for months."

We walked back through the house and I closed all the doors. I sighed in relief when we were back on the museum side. I walked with them out to the patio and she gazed out to the lighthouse. "Is there still a lighthouse keeper?" she asked.

I told her that unfortunately, no, it was now automatic and turned on by itself when the sun went down.

"What a shame. I have so many lovely memories of the lighthouse keeper of Cavalleria. My sister and I rode a donkey every day to the lighthouse, and the lighthouse keeper would teach us reading, writing and arithmetic."

I walked with them out to the car park. They all thanked me and, when the eighty-eight-year-old woman thanked me, I honestly said, "No, I would like to thank you."

She smiled understanding, gave my arm a soft pat and let her family help her into the car. As they drove off, I could see that she was lost in her happy memories.

*   *   *   *

Fernando studied archaeology in Barcelona and among his class was Toni from Menorca. During their studies, a grant was offered to the best project presented focusing on the development of an abandoned or unstudied Roman site. The grant was more focused at tenured professors, but that did not stop Fernando, as nothing does. He asked Toni if he knew of such a site in Menorca, and Toni said that yes, there was a site in the north that a Menorcan archaeologist had started and abandoned because of lack of funding and also because she claimed the site to be unimportant.

"Perfect," Fernando said.

Toni seemed less optimistic, but tagged along. Fernando met with the owner, who granted permission to excavate on his land because of his love for archaeology. He spoke with the heritage department and they said they saw no problem in his excavating there if he won the grant, as he was already a licensed archaeologist furthering his knowledge with graduate studies. He spoke with the previous archaeologist, who now worked in the heritage department, and she said she thought it was great and would just like to be included in the project in some way. So Fernando wrote up the project and, lo and behold, won the grant.

They carried out the research that they had proposed in the project, but Fernando wanted more. Cavalleria had captured him. He kept staring at the abandoned house of Santa Teresa and decided to talk with the owner about it.

He went again to visit the land owner, Señor Olivar, to talk about the possibilities of creating a museum with the artifacts that they found while excavating the Roman city of Sanisera. Fernando told me he was intimidated by the palace where Señor Olivar lives, which is directly in front of and made in a similar fashion to the cathedral of

Ciutadella. He was led into Señor Olivar's office by a servant and noticed the frescos on the ceiling. Señor Olivar was sitting in a stately chair by the fireplace with a brandy snifter in one hand while he gently stroked his hunting dog's head with the other. Fernando said the scene was from out of a movie, and was glad that he was so nervous so that he did not laugh. "Tell me about yourself," Señor Olivar commanded Fernando.

So Fernando began and told him about his hopes to open a type of museum called an Ecomuseum that taught people about the culture and natural heritage of an area. He told Señor Olivar that this museum had to be near the actual place so that people could connect with it and Santa Teresa would be the ideal place for this Ecomuseum.

After six months of visits to Señor Olivar's palace, he agreed that Fernando could use the half of the house that was previously dedicated to the livestock and servants' quarters, with the condition that Fernando fix everything up with his own money and do the yearly maintenance on his side of the house. Fernando was ecstatic because that was what he had wanted, the side with the view of the sea. The front side of the house was separated from the back by a large stone wall, which meant that Fernando could use the entire terrace that faced the sea.

Restoration of the sea-side of Santa Teresa was not easy. There was barbwire randomly coiled around the pine trees, a fig tree growing out of the side of the house, rotten wooden roof beams and cracking walls, not to mention cow, horse, bird and pig shit covering the floor of what was to become the museum.

When everything was finally ready, the heritage department said that they did not feel comfortable having archaeological pieces in a privately run establishment. Fernando almost went crazy, but found a part in the Spanish law dealing with patrimony saying that archaeological piece should be exhibited as near to the archaeological site as possible. This saved Fernando and he proceeded with the inauguration of the museum.

In 1994, it was opened to the public. Fernando put out wooden tables and chairs under the pine trees, facing the sea, where people could relax to calming music coming from hidden speakers.

The museum was a success, but was not able to pay workers and fund archaeological excavations in the area, which was what Fernando wanted to do. He started an archaeology field school, advertising by hanging posters up in different Spanish universities. This was unheard of in Spain... charging people to excavate? He received many criticisms, but enough people signed up to fund the excavation. It worked for a while until people started realizing that it was cheaper to participate in the course, which included housing and food, than to stay in Menorca tourist-style. Soon, people who had no interest in archaeology began to sign up just for a cheap place to stay in Menorca. Fernando could not raise the price because he knew that Spaniards would not pay more, but he was not making enough money with the field school to continue on with the excavations. He became fed up and decided to stop the field school and consequently the excavations.

In 2003, I met Fernando and decided to work a summer in the museum before finishing my last year of college. He told me about the past field school and I said that I thought it would work on an international level. We tried it out the following summer and only fourteen people signed up. The following year, we had over seventy participants. The year after that, we jumped to one hundred and forty and had to put people on waiting list. The field school is now more productive than the museum and Fernando has so much research he cannot keep up with it. We now offer three programs: underwater archaeology, the Roman city dig and the necropolis dig. Our students come from all over the world and I am pleased to say that I think the vast majority thoroughly enjoy the course. I remember a physical anthropology student coming back from the field grinning with a Roman skull in her hands. She looked at me with bright eyes and said, "I am having the best time of my life. Never have I learned so much!"

I thought it a bit weird that an old skull could produce this reaction... but to each their own.

* * * *

I am now known as the Yankee who works in the Ecomuseum. We call our staff 'the dysfunctional family of Cavalleria'. We are not sure why, but you have to be weird to work in the museum. All normal people don't last. Nicolas is a perfect example of this.

Fernando needed a maintenance man to pull weeds, whitewash the museum, fix fallen walls, cut up fallen trees, etc. He put an ad in the paper and got a few calls. Nicolas' mom called and arranged an interview time. Fernando was sick of doing interviews. Everyone said that they could do everything and vowed that they would love to work there. When Fernando asked Nicolas why he would like to work there, Nicolas replied, "To be completely honest, I don't like to work... anywhere. My mom made me come to this interview. I'll work if I have to, but if there is someone else interested in the job, you should pick him."

Fernando could not help but laugh and was at least glad that the monotony of the interviews had been broken.

The first maintenance man who promised he could do everything couldn't. Fernando had to show him how to mix lime with water for whitewashing, how to mix cement and how to use a chain saw for cutting fallen trees. He lasted two weeks and then stopped showing up. Fernando called his second choice. This guy knew a bit more, but was constantly too drunk or too stoned to do it. He lasted less than a week. Fernando was sick of it. He bitterly thought that the guys who promised to do everything were all liars and decided to call the one guy who was at least honest: Nicolas. He fit right into our weirdness and is still working at the museum today.

People associate me with the museum and I am usually called on to give reports of the north. One hot day, I was able to escape midday and treat myself to a *menú* in Es Mercadal. It took me a while to grasp the concept of *menú*. Many restaurants offer one during the day. Basically, it is a meal with a set price, usually cheap. I liked *Las Vegas* in Es Mercadal because you get three choices of a first course, three choices of a second course, dessert, bread and wine all for the price of 8€. At some restaurants, the food is more geared towards people who do physical labor, lots of carbohydrates and fried things. However, this is not the case en *Las Vegas*. Yes, there was always a very filling choice, but the food was always excellent considering the price and the place is always full of people during midday. I sat down and was handed *la carta*. I said that I did not need it because I was going to have the *menú* of the day. The waiter rattled off the different options and I happily made my choices. When I was relaxed sipping on a glass of wine, the waiter came up to me and asked, "So how's Santa Teresa?"

I did not recognize him, but I knew from the name that he chose to give the north that he either hunted there or had worked or lived there in the past. I assured him that Santa Teresa was just fine.

"I was up there just the other day looking for asparagus. Did you know that I grew up in that house?"

I had no idea, and I always loved meeting people who had been raised in Santa Teresa. I told him that Señor

Olivar had just been up there the other day and was still going strong at 90.

"I am glad to hear it, though I never liked him much."

This surprised me because I like Señor Olivar very much. He always seemed easy to talk to and fun to joke with.

"It is nothing personal, but my mom worked cleaning Santa Teresa and my dad worked the land. When Señor Olivar would come to hunt, my dad made me run the two kilometers to open the gate for him. Sometimes I would have to wait for hours. That was before the road was paved and there was still a gate at the very entrance of Cavalleria. I was just a boy and thought, *why the hell can't he open the damn gate for himself?* It made much more sense than having a little boy run two kilometers and wait half of the day to do it for him. I guess it wasn't his fault. Maybe he didn't ask my dad for me to do it, but I still can't shake the resentment that I feel for him."

I said I could understand his feelings. I was always amazed how separated the classes were until very recently in Menorca and how one had to serve the other so completely. I sometimes wondered when I heard stories like this if Menorca was the last place in Spain for feudalism to die.

"But I have more good memories than bad of Santa Teresa. I carry her in my heart. I remember, when I was boy, we always used to play in Cala Viola. It was far enough away from home that we couldn't hear my mom yelling at us if she found some extra work for us to do. Everything in the Mediterranean washes up on that beach. One day, we found a huge, dead sea turtle washed up and we tried to pull it far from the water so it would dry and we could keep its huge shell. The shell was bigger than we were. The thing weighed a ton, but the waters must have reclaimed her anyways. We also found ropes and crates,

but the best find was after a nasty storm with the
tramontana wind blowing at full force. When the storm
receded, we went down to play at Cala Viola and found the
entire beach covered with full cigarette cartons. It took us
five trips to bring our treasure home. For the next few days,
every surface of every stone wall around Santa Teresa was
completely covered with cigarette packs drying in the sun."

I smiled at his story, perfectly imagining it in my head,
and thought to myself that I am seriously one of the
luckiest people alive to be part of such a beautiful place
with so much authentic history.

3

Saint Christopher's Day

My favorite professor came to visit me my first summer here after a conference she attended in Germany. I can usually gage whether people will like Menorca or not, but with Meg I had no idea. She and I had a very comfortable student-professor relationship, but we did not really know each other outside of the world of academia.

She came for four days in July. Normally, this is a wonderful time to come; the weather is mildly hot and there are still not the amounts of tourist that show up in August. The day I went to pick her up at the airport, I noticed that it was unusually hot. I brought her back to my apartment and, for the first time, it dawned on me that there was no way of cooling the house except for opening the windows. I showed Meg her room, opened her window and was assaulted by a gust of scorching wind. We were both dripping sweat from the short walk from the car. I could tell that she was not overly impressed that the only way to control the room temperature was by opening a window to let more hot air in.

"It cools down a lot at night and you can leave your window open."

"But there are no screens.... Don't insects come in?"

"A few, but there are not as many bugs here as there are in California," I lied.

I enjoy immensely the fact that there are no screens on the windows. Nothing gives me more pleasure than sticking my head out the window to watch the summer sun set behind the large palm tree west of my apartment... the smell of rich soil and the bluish clear light of twilight that makes everything glow, giving it a life of its own. In no other place have I noticed how potent and rich the earth smells at twilight as I do here. As if the soil breaths a deep sigh of relief as the punishing Mediterranean sun relinquishes its control to the cool damp night. It reminds me of the smell of the first rains after a long drought. I would hate a screen stopping me from leaning out the window, absorbing all of this, even if it means a few mosquito bites.

One day, a friend who was staying with us had his head stuck out the window watching the sunset and started calling my name frantically. I went running over not knowing what horrible thing to expect.

"Look, look, the green ray... the green ray at sunset!"

I leaned out the window and, indeed, there was a green line coming out of the horizon. "Is this something special like a falling star?" I asked.

A shocked and unbelieving face stared back at me. "Have you never read Jules Verne?"

"No," I confessed. Why is it that I feel more stupid admitting ignorance on a topic to a European than I do to anyone else?

The Green Ray at sunset was then explained to me. We took photos, but none of them showed the beautiful green streak that shot out of the space where the sun was squeezing into the horizon. It is only a memory, and is one of those memories that no one believes, so I did not mention it or any of these positive features that are only provided by screenless windows to Meg. Much easier to lie and say there were not as many bugs.

I took the next day off and decided to take Meg to the most acclaimed and beautiful beach in the north, Pregonda. She had a haggard look to her face that I had not seen before, which led me to suspect that she had not slept well the night before. I had not either. The heat did not let up even after sun set. Sleep was impossible... My body was too busy sweating to sleep.

We put on our swimming suits and headed out. I got in the car and rolled the window down. Meg hesitated before she did the same. I realized that she had probably been hoping for air conditioning in the car... Well, no such luck. We arrived at Binimel·là about a half an hour later.

"You may have noticed that the names of many places start with 'Bini'. This is from the Muslim occupation of the island. 'Bini' means 'son of'," I informed her while pointing to the sign of Binimel·là.

"So this is not Pregonda?"

"No, Pregonda is a twenty-minute walk from here."

Happiness was not the emotion that registered on her face.

We began our walk on a red dirt trail along the northern coast. I had only been to Pregonda once before and made the mistake that the majority of the tourists make... I took the wide trail up the very large hill. The reason that the trail is large and well beaten is because everyone goes up it and then comes directly down when they reach the top and realize there is no way down other than the trail they just hiked up. After correcting this tiring ten-minute mistake, we got back on the correct trail that goes behind the very large hill.

On my previous walk to Pregonda, I had noticed that to the left of the trail about half way to Pregonda was what looked like a hole in the cliff that had been sealed off by a rock wall. There was what seemed to be a doorway or entrance that was not sealed, so I had gone and checked it out. I had seen many structures like this along the northern coast, camouflaged crevasses in the cliffs, and I asked Fernando if he knew what they were.

"Bunkers from Spain's civil war in the 30s. Menorca was the last stronghold of the Republic," he told me. "The anti-Francos," he added quickly, not knowing what my knowledge of Spanish history entailed.

I assumed that this was one of those bunkers. I crossed the field and stepped through the entrance. I was surprised at the size of what seemed to be a cave. Once my eyes adjusted, I saw three stone pillars carved from the natural rock that were narrow on the bottom and became increasingly wider as they reached up and became part of the stone ceiling. I could see marks all along the roof and walls that were made when the cave had been carved out of the *mares,* the typical sandstone found along the coast. I had only seen these kinds of pillars before in a *Talayotic* cave near my town Es Migjorn Gran. I remembered from translating one of Fernando's lectures to the students that, when the first inhabitants of Menorca arrived here, they lived along the coast in caves before they moved into the interior of the island and built more advanced villages and began cultivating the land. The rocks that closed up what would have been a larger entrance looked more recent and I suspected that this cave had, indeed, been used as a bunker in the civil war.

I decided to show Meg this interesting intermingle of two different cultures. The heat was already unbearable when I had this bright idea of extending our hike further to go check out the cave/bunker, but Meg was a trooper and agreed. We crossed the field and were repeatedly cut by dry weeds and stickers.

"Do you think that there are snakes in these weeds?" Meg asked.

"I doubt it," I lied. "Even if there are, there are no poisonous snakes on Menorca."

That did not have the reassuring effect I had hoped for.

We reached the cave and stepped into the entrance. It reeked of urine. There was a stained and holey towel hanging from the wall by a protruding stone and a disgusting, crusty looking mattress on the ground along the far wall.

Meg backed out quickly. "I am not going in there."

"Don't worry; me neither."

As we hiked back across the field of stickers, I told Meg, "Well, you are very lucky... You got to see an interplay of three very different cultures; *Talayotic*, Spanish soldiers and Mediterranean hippies."

She was looking down either at her scratched legs or for snakes and I could tell that she did not buy the part about how very lucky she was.

We came to the small beach before Pregonda and I told Meg that we only had to cross this beach and climb that (very steep) hill that loomed in front of us and we would be in Pregonda. She looked and me, then to the hill, and then back to me again and said, "This beach is fine; why don't we just stay here?"

I really wanted her to see the amazing rock formations that jet out of the water in Pregonda, creating a natural little bay, but I could tell that she did not really care about rock formations at the moment. The heat had gotten worse and the water was very inviting.

"Alright, I am sure if we swim out a ways we will be able to see the angle of the rock formations that you see from Pregonda."

As we approached the water, I prayed, *please, God do not let there be jellyfish.* I was pretty sure that if the water was full of stinging jellyfish, I would be killed on the spot or at least failed next semester. To my profound relief, there were no jellyfish. We immediately took off the clothes that we were wearing over our swimsuits and jumped in. The salt water hitting my fresh cuts from the hike across the field made me yelp out in pain, but the pleasure of finally being cool was enough to override any other sensation. We swam out a ways and admired the rock formations. We were both now much more in the mood for admiring the beauty of nature, which, just minutes before, had been our enemy.

"The water is so clear I can see the bottom perfectly. I am going to see if I can go down and touch it." Meg handed me her glasses, took a deep breath and went under, trying to touch the sand with her fingertips. I knew from anchoring our sailboat that it was pretty deep, around six meters where we were at. So I knew she was not going to make it; however, I expected her to get a lot further than she did. To me, it looked like she hardly left the surface.

When she came up gasping for air, she asked, "How far down did I go?"

I did not have the heart to tell that she had barely left the surface, so instead I said, "I'm not really sure. The water is so clear and the bottom seems so near that my depth perception is totally off."

I got a kind of *whatever* look. "Let's see if you can do better."

I sucked in a good amount of air and struggled downwards with all my force. When I surfaced, Meg was laughing. "You hardly left the surface."

"Well, you didn't either, but I felt bad telling you so."

We both laughed at our incompetence as divers.

"I think it is the salt," I said. "It makes us more buoyant. I feel like my ass is an air mattress."

Meg roared with laughter. Once the semester began again, that would be one of the many quotes on the quote board in Meg's lab where I worked as a researcher.

We floated and swam around for a few hours, then decided to head back. As we were drying off, I was trying to distract Meg with bits of trivial facts of Menorca so that she would not think about the inescapable heat that we now had to face. "The sand in the majority of the northern beaches is a reddish-orange with large sand particles, while the sand in the southern beaches is white and very fine. It has to do with the different minerals in the different parts of the island," I babbled off.

We started our walk back and I felt like I was in one of those stories that are stereotypical of older people that go something like, 'when I was your age, I had to walk to school ten miles in the snow uphill both ways'. It felt like that except that the snow was unbearable heat and the ten miles were only twenty minutes, but there was so much humidity in the air that I felt like I was drowning every time I took a breath, and the uphill both ways felt just like that. I was hoping that I was the only one noticing all of this, but Meg's next comment assured me that I was not.

"Lana, this wonderful red sand with large particles is more difficult to brush off than normal sand and it is rubbing the soles of my feet off."

Note to self: babbling trivial facts can backfire.

"Death march, death march, Lana has taken me on a death march."

I had to agree that this was a very accurate description of what our hike felt like. I am in pretty good shape and I was surprised at how much a twenty-minute hike was affecting me, even if the air had turned to water.

We got into the car, which would be more correctly described as a sauna. When we reached the house, Meg told me that she was going to shower and rest. I took advantage of this time and went to help Fernando, who was running the museum, gift shop and bar alone so that I could take my professor out sightseeing. I felt guilty that he had to do everything alone, which is difficult enough with both of us there. I felt even more guilty when I saw that all of the tables on the terrace of the bar where completely full.

"Holy shit, it is early July; I am surprised that there are so many people," I said to a very tired-looking Fernando.

"It is this heat; no one can stand being at the beach. This is the only shade in the area and people are coming in flocks. The heat has made them half nuts; I thought I was going to be killed by customers twice today when I said I had no ice for their drinks."

"Why don't you have any ice?"

"When I went to the gas station to pick up ice this morning, they told me that there would be no more ice for at least a month because the factory that produces ice on the island broke due to overproduction. The only people who are going to have ice for a while are people who have their own ice machines. He also told me that this is the worst heat wave that anyone can remember. I went to the store to buy ice trays and they were completely sold out. The clerk told me that I was out of luck if I wanted ice trays or fans because they were all sold out and would not be getting more in stock for a while."

"Well at least it's good for business."

"Yeah, and not just for the bar. When people ask what the museum is about, I tell them and add that the exposition is air conditioned. Everyone who has heard that has gone in."

We finished up the work day together and headed home at around 9 pm. When I came through the door, Meg came out of her room to greet me. She had a slightly hysterical look in her eyes.

"So how was your rest?" I asked, even though I was pretty sure I knew the answer.

"Rest? Rest! I took a shower and as soon as I laid down everyone in this town started honking their horns. The whole town! It went on and on for hours and hours. And while this was happening, look what I developed." Meg lifted up the back of her shirt and showed me her back. It was completely covered in little, red, very itchy looking bumps. It was one of the worst cases of heat rash I had ever seen. "Between the itching and the honking..."

"Maybe there was a wedding and they were honking their horns as a farewell to the bride and groom," I offered.

"Well if it was a wedding, the entire town was invited."

I assumed Meg was exaggerating and thought little more of it. After dinner, around 10:30 pm, I heard music coming from the street below. I asked Meg if she would like to go down and see what was going on.

She very enthusiastically declined.

As I walked near the center of town, I found myself in the midst of a celebration. There were streamers crossing all of the narrow cobblestone streets attached from roof to roof above. A stage had been erected in the center plaza in front of the little white church with yellow trim. Hundreds of streamers were attached to the steeple of the church and fanned out over the plaza, streaking the night sky with bright yellows, blues, reds, whites and greens. The band played popular songs while people of Es Migjorn Gran of all ages danced.

I wandered down the pedestrian street that passes the library and *panadería*, where I go in the mornings when I feel I deserve a treat and buy myself a croissant filled with warm chocolate. But the street was much changed from its typical appearance. Apart from all of the streamers above, all the houses on either side of the narrow street had brought out all of their chairs and tables, and bamboo stalks decorated the walls. People were eating wonderful-looking treats. Just as I was about to start drooling, a woman approached me with a tray full of *pastisets*, a flower-shaped cookie covered in powdered sugar. I was reluctant to take one, not knowing what I had done to deserve this goody. She saw my hesitance and shoved the tray closer to me. I took one and thanked her.

While I was munching on my yummy *pastiset*, I wandered by the library. In the doorway, there was a machine that looked like a soda fountain machine. On closer observation, I notice that this machine was only dispensing *pomada*.[3] *Pomada* is the drink of the island. It is made out of the sweet gin made on the island and lemon soda or ideally freshly squeezed lemon (I also like to put in some mint leaves). If possible, it should be put in the freezer. The lemon freezes while the gin just gets cold, resulting in a slushy gin and lemon. It goes down too good, especially on sweltering, humid nights such as what we were experiencing. It is sweet and refreshing, but can give the worse, skull-crushing hangovers imaginable. I made my way to the ingenious *pomada* dispensing machine and was given a plastic cup full.

"How much?"

"It's free."

I was not sure why my *pomada* was free, but I know when not to complicate things and just said, "*Gracias*."

---

[3] While this drink is made the same or similar all over the island, it has two different names. Pomada is what it is called in most parts of the island. However, if one wants this tasty beverage in Ciutadella, one should order a gin and lemon. Ordering a pomada will result in locals telling you to go to the pharmacy for soothing cream (even though they know what you mean) and a very ungenerous portion of gin in your gin y limón.

I saw Nicolas cheerfully making his way to the *pomada* stand. I could tell by his swaying gait and enormous grin that he had been there before.

"Hola Nicolas."

"Hola Lana."

"Can you please tell me why there is a festival in the center of town, why people have all their furniture out in the street, why old women are giving me free *pastisets* and why the library is giving out free *pomada*?"

"Lana, for God's sake," he said in a disbelieving tone, which was high pitched, loud and exaggerated thanks to the free beverages provided by the *biblioteca*. "Today is the town's day."

"Today is Es Migjorn Gran Day?" I asked, not sure I was understanding correctly.

"Yes, of course."

"Does this have anything to do with all of the honking horns today?"

"Of course it does, Lana," Nicolas said to me as if I was slightly mentally challenged. "Of course, it is the day of the town." He said this in a way as if horns honking and it being the day of the town made perfect sense and was perfectly obvious.

I asked for another *pomada* and then wandered back to where the band was playing and watched couples dancing; granddaughters and grandfathers dancing, and small children dancing in groups. I noticed that I was standing near the pharmacist of the town, Lucas, a very nice and easy to talk to kind of person (except when it is about getting a cream for my mushrooms) and I gave him an in the air cheers/greeting with my *pomada*. He wandered over. "Enjoying the festivities?" he asked.

"Yes, though I am not exactly clear as to what they are about."

"It is the town's day."

"I got that part, but I am not sure as to why it is today and why people were honking their horns earlier."

"Ah," he said, and I could tell by his look that he was preparing to fill the poor uncultured North American in. "Today is Saint Christopher's Day. You may have heard locals refer to Es Migjorn Gran as San Cristobal."

I had, in fact. Nicolas always refers to our town as San Cristobal. When I asked Fernando why Nicolas called our town by a different name, he told me that, during Franco's dictatorship, it was prohibited to write and speak Catalan.

"Es Migjorn is the name of the southern wind here in Menorca, and Menorquín is a dialect of Catalan. So, when Franco took power, many towns that had Catalan names began using Spanish names instead. Es Migjorn Gran became San Cristobal. This also happened with names of people and especially with children born during Franco's reign," Fernando had said.

"People were not allowed to give the names that they wanted to their children?" I had asked, unbelieving.

Fernando nodded affirmatively. "For example, remember those two nice guys who came to the museum the other day asking about rock climbing on the island?"

I did, indeed; Gorka and Unai. I remembered because I was expecting more typical Spanish names being that they sounded very Spanish to me. They had seen my surprise at their names and told me they were from the Basque country and that their names were of their language, Euskera, or more commonly referred to as Basque.

"People from my generation in the Basque country, Catalonia and other places where Catalan is spoken," continued Fernando, "all have typical Spanish names because their families were not allowed to name them in their own language. However, people from your generation, born after the dictatorship, can be named in their own language, hence Gorka and Unai."

Because I had been so surprised that both Catalan and Euskera were prohibited – even the names of children – I had forgotten to ask why the town citizens of Es Migjorn Gran had decided upon the name San Cristobal. Listening to Lucas, I remembered that I had never asked.

The pharmacist continued on with his lesson for the poor uninformed foreigner "They called the town San Cristobal because that is the patron saint of our town... Saint Christopher, I believe you say in English." He looked happy that he knew the saint's name in English and looked to me for confirmation, which made me feel even more ignorant because I have no idea about any of the saints. So I just nodded my head in agreement and made a mental note to look it up on the internet.

"So I still do not understand why everyone was honking their car horns."

"Saint Christopher is the patron saint of motorists."

"Of motorists?" I was kind of let down; I had a nice, be it very limited, stereotype of saints and it included timeless things. I am okay with patron saints of the sick, or of lost causes or of women.... but of motorists? I imagined Saint Christopher with a modern neon halo.

"Yes, of motorists. Actually, I believe he is the patron saint of travelers in general, but now that driving has become the most common way to travel, Saint Christopher has been adopted by motorists and that is why everyone was honking their horns today. After *siesta*, everyone gets in their cars, scooters and motorcycles and drive to the church. Once you are in front of the church, you give a donation and the priest sprinkles holy water on your vehicle and blesses it."

"Do you have to give a donation to get your car blessed?" I asked, always suspicious of the church's reasons behind anything.

"I don't think so, but everyone does."

Nicolas, having successfully refilled his *pomada,* wondered over to where we were.

"So, Nicolas, did you go and get your car blessed today?" I asked.

"*Madre de Dios, no.* I did it once a few years back and had to wait in line for over two hours."

"Do people honk their horns the entire time?" I asked, starting to think that maybe Meg had not been exaggerating.

"Yes, and then they drive around town afterward honking their new blessed vehicle."

"And many people bring more than one vehicle to get blessed, so it goes on for quite a while," added Lucas.

"So did you get your scooter blessed, as well?" I mockingly asked Lucas.

He rides his scooter to work every morning and parks it in front of the pharmacy, which is below my apartment. We cross daily, me walking and him on his scooter because I park my car near his house and walk. He stops his scooter daily and good-naturedly lets me hassle him about how ridiculous it is to ride a scooter from his house to the pharmacy, which is only about a 100 meter distance. To this, he always comments that it is a cultural thing that I could not possibly understand. To which I always reply that it is bad for the environment and that a little walk twice a day would be good for his health.

"Of course I did, Lana," he replied, smiling.

I rolled my eyes, which caused his smile to turn into a chuckle. I heard the bells of the church marking the hour above the music and checked my watch. It was already midnight, early by Spanish standards, but I had promised

Fernando that I would go early and open up the museum so that he would have everything ready when I went off on another excursion with my professor. I headed home, leaving the town to their festivities.

I tried to be quiet when I came in, but it did not really matter because no one was asleep. Meg asked through her door, "Is there a party going on below my window?"

"Pretty much, yes."

"And will it be over soon?"

"When I left, there was no indication of that. Goodnight."

"Goodnight," Meg replied, but her tone of voice led me to suspect that she was just using a polite term and that she did not really feel that it was a good night or had any hope of it being one.

The next morning, I could tell that she had not slept much. "So my dilemma last night was this: do not sleep because of the music and people in the street all night, or close my window and suffocate in the heat. I tried both and neither worked very well."

Fernando and I had also tried both and decided for noise instead of death by heatstroke.

I think that Meg enjoyed the next few days on the island, but I am not quite sure that anything made up for Saint Christopher's Day.

*   *   *   *

Exactly one year later, July 10th, I could go no longer. I had no idea that it was one year later, or even what the date was. I had been working seven days a week, ten to fourteen hours straight since Easter. I told Fernando, who was excavating in the Roman military camp with students, that if I did not go home and relax, I was going to drop dead in front of all of the tourist in the middle of the terrace.

"And the new girls? Can they manage?"

"I don't care if they can manage; I am going to die and then they will have to manage all summer instead of just today."

I am sure that Fernando realized that if he objected I was going to cut his head off, and opted for the easiest solution. I am also sure he took into account that I don't complain unless I really need to.

"Okay, go home and rest. Tell the girls that if they have any questions and if they can't get to me here, they should call you."

"Fine," I said over my shoulder as I walked to my car, turning my cell phone off.

The drive home seemed eternal. I was never going to get home, never going to take a shower, and never going to lie down and relax. Just when I was about to give up hope, Es Migjorn Gran appeared on the horizon like an oasis. I dragged my tired body up the stairs to my apartment. I started undressing in the hallway, leaving my clothes where they fell. I felt like a new being as the hot water of the shower pounded down on my tired muscles. I thought that I heard noises while in the shower… an alarm clock? I stuck my head around the curtain a few times, but nothing in the house seemed amiss. I stayed in the shower until the hot water ran out, something that I would never do if Fernando was home. Water is a very precious resource in Spain, and especially in Menorca, where there are no lakes or rivers. Fernando is annoyingly not hypocritical in his water conservation hysteria. When he takes a shower, he rinses, shuts the water off, lathers up and then turns the water back on to rinse off the soap and shampoo. I admire this dedication to water conservation; however, I was not really in the mood to care.

After I drained the hot water, I was toweling off when I realized that the noises I had been hearing while in the shower were coming from outside. I had a flashback to Meg's hysterical eyes and thought to myself, *NNNNNNOOOOOOOOOO*. But, of course, the answer was yes. It was once again Saint Christopher's Day; however, I was the one now in desperate need of rest. The horns blared outside. I had no idea the amount of noise that a town full of horns honking all at once could make. I lay down on my bed and cursed everything that I could think of to curse. There was no way to relax with all the racket. Meg had not been exaggerating.

Centuries later, I heard Fernando come through the door. I felt I had that slightly hysterical look in my eyes that Meg had had. The horns had stopped honking by then, so my husband had no idea what I had been through. He sweetly asked, "Do you feel better after your rest?"

I answered, "I hope Saint Christopher was the one who was crucified upside down."

"No, that was Saint Peter, the founder of the church," my always-helpful husband replied.

"Whatever!"

4

Hunting and Gathering

It seems that for each month of the year there is something the Menorcan land or surrounding water gives to its people as a special gift. Game birds so fat they can hardly fly, rabbits, snails, wild asparagus, camomile, rosemary, mushrooms of all shapes and sizes, and an unbelievable abundance of fish and shellfish, are just a few of things that I have been shown how to find, prepare and enjoy.

Because there are no large, wild animals on the island, hunting is limited to mainly rabbits and game birds. A typical island hunting scene is the same now as many oil paintings portray it to have been years ago; men, rifles and dogs. Whenever I am driving some windy country road and pass hunters out in the field with their eager pointers, I feel that I am peeking into the past, seeing one of the oil paintings that I have studied on the walls of Menorcan noble families' antique homes come to life. From what I have been told, hunting seems more of a hobby or sport here, where fishing and gathering are of much greater consequence.

Nothing is more beautiful than seeing a lone fisherman coming back in his *llaüt* in the last light of day. This typical Menorcan finishing boat is small and wooden with a 'squarish' sail in the middle. I cannot conjure up an image of the Mediterranean without this small boat afloat a turquoise sea. Before tourism on the island, fishing was a cornerstone of Menorcan life. Now, there are only a few men who continue the trade as a way of life.

Watching the fishermen in the north in either the port of Fornells or in Sanitja is one of the few ways one can travel back in time and see what Menorca was like before. In Fornells, fishermen often take a *ginet*, a shot of the local gin, to warm up their blood before going out to sea.

Many fishermen go after *la langosta*. In any Menorcan recipe book, one can find the recipe for the *caldereta de langosta*. This scraggily, spinney lobster was what the fisherman kept to eat, selling all of the *good* catch. Because of the little amount of meat on the lobsters in the area, they had to make a soup out of it. Now this plate that was once for poor fishermen goes for 60€ per person or more in any of the many restaurants that serve it. I have only tried the *caldereta de langosta* once when my husband lost a bet to Nicolas, the prize being this plate for the three of us. I admit it was a nice dish. The broth was wonderfully rich. However, 60€ a plate is a bit much for what it is. But it is one of the 'things to do while in Menorca'. Personally, it is not something that I would spend that amount of money on more than once.

Men also spearfish and fish from the rocks. Most people who spearfish have an amazing lung capacity. Nicolas says that he can go down twenty meters with weights, but without the aid of a tank. I have never witnessed this, so I cannot verify his claim, but I have been told that many locals can do it.

Fishing from the rocks is something that I have done and do not enjoy. Mainly, you catch rock-fish, which are small, colorful fish that Menorcans use to make soup. Nicolas took me once and I could not justify the amount of rock-fish that must be killed to make a pot of soup. To

Nicolas' great frustration, every time he was not looking, I would throw all the ones I had caught back into the water. He wanted to help me unhook my catch each time, but I noticed that he squeezed them so hard while unhooking them that there was no chance of them having a happy ending. Of course, Nicolas at first did not know that I was throwing them back, and being that he never ever throws anything back, he gives no thought to how he treats them while he unhooks them.

One of my favorite misunderstandings was a fishing-related event and happened when Nicolas announced that he was going to make a *paella* for Fernando and me.

"Everything in the *paella* is going to be something that I caught, found or grew," Nicolas informed us. "So I have to get off work early today so I have plenty of time to get an abundant catch so your Yankee girl will have a proper first *paella*," he said, looking hopefully at Fernando.

Fernando mumbled something as he walked off about fine, but he should not use making us a *paella* as an excuse to get off work early to go fishing.

"What are you going to put in the *paella*?" I eagerly asked.

He rattled off a few different vegetables and shellfish. In the shellfish category, he mentioned *cangrejo*, which is crab. I questioned him about this because I understood *conejo*, which is rabbit. He said, "Yes, *cangrejo* (which I still understood to be rabbit). The trick is, if you do not use them right after you catch them, to put them in the freezer while they are still alive and that way they do not lose all of their juices."

I imagined poor little bunnies in his freezer shivering to death with their poor floppy ears all hard and frozen. Of course, I freaked out. "Nicolas, I am never, ever going to eat anything that you prepare, you sick, cruel freak!"

Nicolas looked at me like I was crazy and said, "But Lana, it is the most humane way to kill them... Would you prefer me to throw them into a pot of boiling water?"

At this point, I called Nicolas a few very bad names and repeated my vow never again to eat his food, and added that I never wanted to speak to him again. Poor Nicolas walked away with a look of total bewilderment on his face. As the day dragged on, I was plagued with images of poor shivering bunnies. Nicolas finished his shift, and waved goodbye as I glared at him. When I saw Fernando, I told him my vow of not eating Nicolas-prepared food. I explained to him that he put poor little bunnies in the freezers to kill them so that they would taste better. He looked at me strangely and asked, "*Conejos o cangrejos?*"

As soon as he said it, I realized my mistake. I called Nicolas' cell, but only got his voice mail. I left a message explaining that I thought he put little rabbits in the freezer. I told him that I could understand doing this with crabs and that I hoped that he could understand my reaction thinking it was rabbits instead of crabs. I apologized and said that I hoped he would still prepare *paella* for us. The next day, he came to work with the biggest grin on his face. He loved my message. He said, "I explained to half the town that the crazy American thought I put live rabbits in the freezer."

That night, we had the most wonderful *paella*. Nicolas picked one of the crab legs out of the rice and said, "First, you suck the juice of the leg, then you crack it with your teeth and suck out the rest of the juice." As I did this, with juice dripping down my fingers and chin, Nicolas said, "And the reason that there is so much juice is because I put these poor little rabbits in the freezer while they were still alive."

*   *   *   *

Gathering is big on the island, especially among older, retired men. In March and April, you will see old men riding on their scooters through the wild flowers with plastic bags or newspapers rolled in a funnel form full of wild asparagus. The wild asparagus on the island are very tough and chewy. I have steamed them to no end and only the very tips do not threaten to break teeth.

During these months, Nicolas often wonders off for fifteen to twenty minutes and comes back with two huge hands full of wild asparagus. I asked him if he would show me what a wild asparagus plant looks like. The first thing the plant made me think of was gloves. It is a spiky, dark green plant and, of course, the asparagus stocks start from the center and are protected by the rest of this evil plant. Hunting for asparagus reminds me of those computer-generated pictures that were popular in the 90s that, when you stared at them long enough and maybe a bit cross-eyed, a previously hidden picture popped out. I was never able to make these pictures pop out until one day when I was exhausted from an adolescent 'shopathon' with my friend. I walked past a store window where several of these pictures were displayed and each and every one of the hidden images popped out for my tired eyes. Ever since that day, all the hidden images in these pictures automatically pop out for me without even making an effort. Asparagus hunting is like this. I was so frustrated at first because I knew that there were many plants around the museum, because Nicolas would effortlessly return with the proof. However, even when I found a plant, I could find no more than one or two scrawny stalks.

Then, one day in late March, I found a plant and calmly poked around. At first, I thought that it had two stalks, then I noticed three, then five until I had sixteen stalks from just one plant. After that experience, wild asparagus stalks pop out for me.

Nicolas told me that he gets a euro for each asparagus bunch he sells. I was curious as to what one would do with these wild asparagus because my steaming and roasting efforts had yielded only very stringy and very hard results. "The most common thing to do with wild asparagus in Menorca is to put them in an omelet. My mom also makes a really good soup with them. She throws into a pot of water the asparagus, some *dientes* of garlic, onions, salt and olive oil and lets it boil for a while, first with a high flame and them turning it down once it starts to boil. *Sopa oliaigua* is what it is called. You usually pour it over some dried bread. Very good. In summer, after asparagus season, she makes a similar soup, substituting the asparagus for figs and adding tomato sauce."

*   *   *   *

On May mornings, there is usually a line of at least five cars going about twenty kilometers per hour behind various old men on scooters wearing rubber boots with a plastic bucket either hooked in the crook of their arm or somehow attached to their vehicle. This is the official *caracol* or land-snails-getting attire. In May, there is a good amount of moisture on the ground early in the day and the *caracoles* climb up the various plants to escape the moisture. This makes them easy prey for old men equipped with rubber boots so as to not be bothered by the moisture and a plastic bucket to collect the snails in.

On rainy days, the country roads are lined with vehicles belonging to people collecting *caracoles* that escape drowning by taking refuge on the road... Not the best of ideas. *Caracoles* and their collectors have often caused me near-death experiences. Many of the country roads in Menorca are very windy, narrow and full of potholes. I would not change these roads for anything... They give

Menorca its rural feel and charm. However, they are not the safest roads to travel on... especially in the rain. When it rains, these roads become very slick and even more potholes emerge. More than once, I have turned a narrow corner and almost run over a Menorcan in a rain poncho and rubber boots holding a plastic bucket. If it is not the person itself, it is the parked, more often semi-parked, car that forces me to swerve, break, skid and hit potholes bigger than my car. It is a good thing that Renault 4s are indestructible.

On rainy days when no one is out looking for *caracoles*, I almost kill myself driving all the same because I feel so guilty running over the hundreds of *caracoles* on the road. Hearing their fragile little shells crunch beneath my tires, I often do not watch where I am going and only pay attention to where to swerve to kill the least amount. This is not the safest thing to do because the place on the road where there is inevitably the least amount of *caracoles* is the other side of the road right before a blind curve.

Once, when an old man was collecting *caracoles* near the museum, I asked him how he prepares them. He said, "First, you get a bag that lets air in, like a burlap sack, or you can even use one of those bags that onions come in, and you put all the *caracoles* in the bag and hang the bag up for a few days. The reason you do this is so they can clean themselves out." I guess that I had a confused look on my face because he added, "No eating and only shitting is how they clean themselves out. After a few days, they are good to eat. I sauté mine in olive oil with diced onions and fresh tomato sauce."

I have eaten *caracoles* prepared in a similar manner. They are not my favorite dish, but I will eat them if offered to me. I also feel that I have to eat them to prove myself. My husband does not eat *caracoles*; he thinks they are gross. If he does not eat them, people just assume he does not like *caracoles*. However, if I do not eat them, people make a point of calling attention to the fact that the Yankee is not eating them, and then inevitably I will be offered, to everyone else's great amusement, a hamburger. So I always eat the *caracoles*. But, I do not have the heart to prepare them. When the old man got to the part about hanging them up all together in a bag for a few days with no food, I decided that this was one typical Menorcan dish that I was not going to prepare. I tried to rationalize with myself, explaining to myself that there is no difference between running over hundreds in my car, to stopping and picking them up and hanging them for a few days. But I do not think I could sleep knowing that there were hungry little *caracoles* awaiting their deaths, hanging in my kitchen. Yes, this makes me a bit of a hypocrite. I don't necessarily protest their suffering (because I eat them); I just don't want them to suffer in front of me. Nicolas has informed me that *caracoles* are not capable of suffering... but I still can't do it.

*   *   *   *

As May rolls over to June, the majority of the wild flowers wilt away in the early summer sun and their numerous colors are replaced by the golden of drying plants dotted with the red of *amapolas*, the corn poppy, which outlast other wildflowers, battling the summer heat until July and even August. In the north of the island, bright yellow accompanies the reds and goldens of early summer. Menorcan camomile, another gift from the land, engulfs the Cape of Cavalleria and La Mola with its pure and refreshing aroma.

In Cavalleria, it is a protected species, but that is something this foreigner would never tell the old men who collect it there. How could I explain to someone who has been collecting Menorcan camomile his entire life that it cannot be done because it is now protected, surely thanks to people like me who have raised the population of Menorca to that where gifts from the land and water have to be protected so as to not become endangered or extinct. This is also why I don't launch into my typical green speech when Nicolas explains to me some of his not-so-legitimate fishing endeavors.

Another reason that I do not confront the elderly men who come to Cavalleria to collect camomile in large quantities is that they are usually armed. My mother had an unfortunate encounter with one such man that left her quite shaken until I finally got the story out of her and was able to explain the situation. It was June and she decided to walk from the museum to the lighthouse, a nice and tranquil three-kilometer walk. On the way back, she veered off the road and went exploring on different goat paths. After walking around one of the few large pine trees on the cape, she came upon the Grim Reaper.

"He had a horribly curved blade that was mounted on a long staff and a huge burlap sack that could easily fit a human body."

I was so surprised by this unlikely story that I did not initially realize what she had seen.

"I quickly turned and walked towards the road as fast as I could without breaking into a run. He kept on his goat path, but kept looking at me in a strange way every few seconds until I was out of sight."

My mom's ashen face was the only thing that kept me from busting up laughing when I finally realized what she had come across. I had never seen anyone cut Menorcan camomile, but I have seen people cut lavender using similar tools and was told that camomile was cut in a similar fashion. Experienced cutters, I had been told and later witnessed, can cut off a surprising amount of blossoms from the bush and deposit them in the burlap sack in one swift motion, swooping with the scythe and open burlap sack. Because camomile blossoms do not weigh much, it is not difficult to carry a burlap, body sized sack full. I am sure that he kept looking at her 'in a strange way', because he was doing something illegal and was nervous as to why this woman kept *looking at him.*

Just to check before I put all my mother's fears to rest, we went walking down a goat path where I knew we would find Menorcan camomile bushes and, sure enough, of the five bushes that we came upon, three fourths of the blossoms had been scythed off each. I felt better now knowing that it was, indeed, a camomile hunter and not the Grim Reaper or a psychopath that my mother had encountered.

Thinking that my mom's stomach might be a wee bit upset, I picked a few blossoms from each bush (not wanting to leave one totally naked) and took them back up to the museum to make tea. Menorcan camomile tea not only has a wonderfully soothing aroma, but also has a wonderfully soothing effect on an upset stomach.

While we were sipping at our tea, I explained to my mom another use for camomile that a Menorcan woman told me about. She uses half of her boiled camomile for tea and the other half she pours into a spray bottle and uses it as a mister on hot days. "Not only is the mist refreshing on a hot face, but it is also very good for the complexion," she had said.

After sharing this tidbit with my mom, who was already very pleased with the calming of her stomach, she was ready to go camomile hunting herself. We hiked many goat trails that day and came upon a few un-pillaged bushes. We did not take three fourths of the blossoms, but only enough to make a bit more tea and to try out our new refreshing and complexion-enhancing mist.

Next to one of the camomile bushes, I pointed out a rosemary bush. I rolled one of the needle-like leaves in my fingers, raised them to my nose and inhaled deeply. My mom followed suit and we added a few rosemary branches to our spoils. Perfect to sprinkle on an oven roasted chicken and potatoes, followed by a relaxing conversation and more soothing tea.

*   *   *   *

Of all the gathering that goes on in the island, nothing compares to *seta* hunting. Mushroom hunting takes place mainly in November, and not only are they a preferred local dish, they can also get you 30€ a kilo on the island. There is a saying in Menorca: 'rain in August; setas in November'. Every time it rains in August, I look at Nicolas, then up at the sky and ask, "You know what this means?"

This is always followed by Nicolas repeating the saying with a big smile and then us doing a little jig, which usually ends in us giving a toast to the August rain.

During my first year in Menorca, Nicolas prepared for me a dish of *robellones* (a word that I cannot pronounce, so I usually stick to the more general term of *setas*), the most sought after type of *seta* on the island. I must admit that I was less than enthusiastic about trying mushrooms that Nicolas had found in the forest. When Nicolas said that he was going to bring a bag full over and prepare them in my house, I looked to Fernando pleadingly for an excuse as to why we could not do this. But, to my dismay, Fernando was very excited about the idea.

One of my first memories is of my mom telling me to never touch wild mushrooms because some were so poisonous that, if you touched them and then put your fingers in your mouth, you could die. This may have been one of those parent exaggerations to get your child's attention... but it sure worked. I felt as though I was planning on partaking in some evil taboo all day, while the hour of eating wild mushrooms drew nearer. I imagined my mother's great disappointment when she was told that my death had been caused by eating wild mushrooms. My mother's tear-streaked face as she told friends and relatives, 'I just don't understand... I always warned her about the dangers of wild mushrooms'.

After work, I dutifully went out and bought two bottles of red wine, which was declared as my contribution to this joyous event. I showered and then ate a lot of bread... my reasoning being that the bread would absorb some of the poison, allowing me a few precious extra minutes to get to the hospital. Nicolas showed up at 9 pm as planned with a few cloves of garlic, fresh parsley and the dreaded bag full of *robellones*. They looked, to me, like little portabellas, a meaty kind of mushroom. Nicolas explained, "You do not rinse them, but brush off the remains from the forest." At which point he produced a narrow brush that looked like a small painting bush and brushed off the dirt and pine needles.

Perfect, I thought. Not only was I going to eat the evil wild mushrooms, but they were not even going to be properly cleaned first.

Nicolas held the stem of a mushroom out to me. "The ends have no dirt on them because *seta* hunters always carry knives so that they cut the mushroom, not yank it out." He produced from his back pocket a multi-use pocketknife and pulled the blade out. It looked as if it was covered in blood. He asked, "Do you see this...? Do you see this?" He was implying the blood-like substance.

I meekly replied '*si*', not knowing Nicolas very well yet and having no idea where he was going with this.

He said, "This, this is how you know you have a *robellon*; they bleed when you cut them. The reason that you should cut and not pull is because they grow back within a week and you can go back and get a whole new load."

He put away his pocket knife, grabbed one of our kitchen knives and began quartering the mushrooms. "It is very important that you cut them before cooking them because some seem to be perfect on the outside and are full of worms and rot on the inside." And, sure enough, he halved one and it looked like cork on the inside. "You see that? That is where the worms have been and it is all full of worms and worm shit. Only keep parts of the mushroom that are whole, meaty and bleed."

This just kept getting better and better... not cleaned, worms...

After we had separated out all of the worm gotten parts of the mushrooms, Nicolas heated up some olive oil in a large pan. He dumped the quartered pieces in and covered it. "We will leave it on low for a while and, when you can smell the juices of the mushrooms escaping, we will add in some diced garlic and parsley. And why is my glass empty?"

I drank lots of wine, hoping for liquid courage. A bit later, much to my surprise, I noticed I was taking deeper and deeper breaths, trying to better smell the amazing earthy aroma that was coming from the kitchen. Nicolas told me to follow him for the next step. He took off the top of the pan and I was surrounded with a smell that made my mouth water. "Look, do you see how there is a light reddish juice? That is the blood of the mushroom. We do not want to cook them too much or they will be dry and chewy... We want them to be soft and meaty." He added in the garlic and parsley, stirred it around with a wooden spoon and we waited a few minutes more, and Nicolas deemed it *seta* eating time.

He brought out the pan and placed it in the center of the table. All of my previous misgivings about eating Nicolas' wild mushrooms were erased by the unique and appetizing smell that engulfed me. I stabbed a quartered piece and placed it in my mouth. It was soft to bite down on and had a meaty texture... meat that cuts like butter. I was not able to compare the taste to anything that I had previously tasted. The only word that came to mind was amazing. I gave Nicolas the thumbs up sign and decided that I was going to become a *seta* addict.

When Nicolas saw how much I was enjoying his forest spoils, he asked me if I would like to go *seta* hunting with him. I was so happy and honored that he asked me. I had heard that *seta* hunters were very secretive about their hunting techniques and places, and I had been preparing to beg Nicolas before he so graciously asked. "Tomorrow, wear long sleeves, pants and boots. I will swing by around 10 am. Bring a knife and a plastic bag."

Nicolas rang the doorbell at 10:37 am. I knew that most people went very early in the morning and let Nicolas know my concern. He laughed and said, "I have been hunting *setas* since I was born. When you are as good as I am, you can go whenever you want. Anyway, they can't get them all, can they?"

So, with this in mind, Nicolas told me that we had to get a coffee with milk before we set off. I drank my coffee down in one gulp and anxiously watched Nicolas sip his coffee. Years later, Nicolas finished his coffee with milk and we finally began our *seta* hunting adventure.

I was expecting that we would hike deep into the forest, but Nicolas informed me that that is what everyone does and it is too much work. "There are enough pine trees and bushes near the road; why complicate things?"

As my romantic image of *seta* hunting deep in the forest evaporated, I bravely tried to replace it with the logic of what Nicolas was saying. I rationalized to myself that, if we stayed near the road, we could hit a lot more spots than by walking half a day to just get to one.

We headed south and parked in the parking lot of a hotel. "Son Bou has great *seta* hunting because it is very humid on the south of the island and the *tramontana* wind does not reach here with the force that it does in the north, which dries out the *setas*." About five feet from the asphalt is where my *seta* hunting class began. "See this scraggily, young pine tree? See the bush underneath it? I'm liking this as a *seta* growing place. Go look around the bush and tell me if you see anything."

I eagerly shoved my face in the bush and scanned the ground. To my great disappointment, I only saw pine needles. Nicolas saw my sad face and came over to take a look in the bush. He made a surprised sound in the back of his throat (Menorcans are great at making throat noises) and said, "No *setas*? I see four at first glance."

I excitedly shoved my head back in the bush, looked intensely around and replied with mounting frustration, "There are no freaking *setas* in here."

Nicolas gave me a big grin and said, "Look where my finger is pointing. Do you see that the pine needles are kind of like a tent? I bet you a 100 Euros that it is a *seta* pushing up from underneath."

I did not take the bet and, sure enough, when Nicolas brushed the pine needles away, there was a perfect little *seta*. He cut it off and covered the red stump back up. "Always cover the stumps back up because *setas* always grow in the same place and if someone sees the bloody stumps, they will know that *setas* grow here and will be back within the week to ravage your spot."

We cut the rest of the *setas* that were hiding under the pine needles, covered up the stump and plopped them into our plastic bag. "You will see that many people use a wicker basket for collecting *setas*. They do this because they say it lets the *setas* spread their spores while they walk around the forest looking for more." He made a throat noise implying *whatever*. "A plastic bag is easier to carry."

We hit other spots as well, getting about four or five *setas* from each spot. By the time we were done, we had nearly a bag full. To my delight, Nicolas handed me the bag. "Here, take these."

I tried to object, saying, "You should get the spoils of the day because you were nice enough to take me and teach me where and how to look for *setas* and I really appreciate it."

"Take the measly little bag full; I am going home to get a large bucket and go to my real *seta* hunting places. Not even my brothers know where they are."

5

Living to be Two Hundred and Thirty

In Es Migjorn Gran, we boast the oldest man (that records can prove) in Europe. He was one hundred and fourteen years old and lucid when he finally passed away gently in his sleep after doing his daily bicycle ride around the town. His younger siblings also made it easily past the century mark. A relative of the oldest man in Europe told me that, when he hit one hundred, the mayor of the town gave him a plaque and said he would continue this new tradition every year on his birthday to celebrate life after one hundred. When he turned one hundred and ten, the mayor asked him if he really wanted another plaque. He responded with a chuckle, "No, what I would really like is a party." From what I heard, it was quite a party, with all of Es Migjorn Gran enthusiastically participating.

My town often makes me think of Gabriel García Marquez's novel, *One Hundred Years of Solitude*. Es Migjorn Gran exudes a certain fantasy realism where even living until two hundred and thirty years of age seems possible.

I believe the reason there seems to be so many more old people in Es Migjorn Gran (and the island in general) than young is due to the fact that they never die. People easily

live forever, or close to it, on the island. I was recently in
the cemetery of Es Migjorn Gran. I like visiting cemeteries.
It makes me feel good to see how people continue to love
after death. Cemeteries speak volumes about the people of
an area and I am always eager to learn about my current
surroundings. I had been in the cemetery many times,
smiling at the fresh flowers, surprised by the *Talayotic*
grinding stones in the well-kept garden, and touched by the
red candles that never go out. But, on this trip, for the first
time, I did the math: ninety-one, ninety-six, ninety-four,
one hundred and five, ninety-two, eighty-six, eighty-seven,
one hundred and one, ninety-four, ninety-nine, eighty-three,
one hundred and two, ninety-five, ninety-seven, etc. How
could that be possible? Most of these people died many
years ago... long before modern-day, life-prolonging
medicines and adequate health care reached the island, yet
they almost *all* neared or passed the century mark.

*   *   *   *

Old women dominate the supermarkets. Old men dominate
the roads. The stereotypical sweet Spanish *abuela* only
exists in her house once her shopping has been conducted.
When she is out buying groceries, everything changes. Old
Menorcan women in the supermarket, bread store, butcher
shop, pharmacy and vegetable and fruit stand are a danger
to the younger public, especially to foreigners who do not
know to get out of the way. The most dangerous time to be
out shopping is between 8:30 am and 12 pm. More than
once, I have been gathering a bag of vegetables and been
shuffled out of the way by an elderly woman wanting the
same vegetable or one near it. The first time this happened
to me, I tried to give the *anciana* the benefit of the doubt...
Maybe she had no peripheral vision and maybe, because of
the multiple layers of sweaters she was wearing during

summer, she did not realize that she just totally bumped me out of the way. However, after repeated occurrences followed by piercing looks suggesting that I was at fault for, God forbid, being in the way, I realized that this had nothing to do with limited vision or anything of the sort. It took a long time, but I have finally come to accept the fact that old women will ram you in the supermarket if you are in their way.

At first, I thought that this particular supermarket behavior might have something to do with me being a foreigner; a semi-subtle way of letting me know that, while I might be tolerated, I was certainly not welcome. Like many US citizens in foreign countries, I feel that everything that happens to me has to do with the fact that I am American and everybody in the world hates us for it. I find myself interpreting all actions with this complex ever present. Sometimes it holds true. For example, I am sure that the bitchy girl in the checkout stand of the supermarket next to my house who asks for ID every time I pay with a credit card does so to make me feel pointedly not welcome.[4] Whereas the old-lady ramming phenomenon

---

[4] This happened during four years. On my fifth year in Es Migjorn Gran, I noticed that the ladies in the local supermarket where not so readily giving out plastic shopping bags; they were no longer set out for the taking – you had to ask. This was annoying because the supermarket by my house has very large and strong plastic bags, which I reused for my plastic recyclable garbage. However, I saw this as an opportunity. The next time I went, I brought my wicker basket and, as I loaded my groceries into it, I said casually, "I noticed that you were trying to save plastic bags, so I decided I would start bringing my basket. Much better for the environment. I think it is great what you guys are doing."

Bitchy launched into a speech about how finally someone noticed and understood. I smiled and handed her my credit card. She swiped it and continued to rant about how other people use ridiculous amounts of bags and thought it was their right to do so… bla bla. I was not asked

was just me being paranoid. I was not able to convince myself of this until the day that I heard '*Ostras*', the Menorcan equivalent of Jesus Christ, in the supermarket. I looked up to see a young local girl about my age looking down with a mixture of surprise and annoyance at a bent old woman who had just severely nudged her to get at the tomatoes. I was so relieved; my thick, blonde hair and ridiculously white smile that scream 'not native' had nothing to do with this curious shopping behavior. I am now okay with being jostled around by little old ladies doing their daily shopping. I even feel more included when it happens[5].

The one thing that I think I will never get used to is the disregard of the line, which almost all Spaniards and especially old women are guilty of. To my great frustration as someone born and raised in the USA, who was taught from birth that order and rules must be followed, the fact that the line is an ambiguous concept is enough to almost send me over the edge. However, for an older woman doing her daily shopping, there is no ambiguity whatsoever about the line; it does not exist. Time spent waiting has no relevance on who will be served next. It seems more dependent on how many old women enter the store behind you yelling out what they want. I was amazed to see that this worked. With my North American naiveties firmly in place, I thought that good turn-taking behavior would be

---

for my ID that day or any day since. Bitchy, who is around my age, even came up and hugged me during the festivals a few weeks later. Granted, she was drunk, but I appreciated the gesture and no longer call her Bitchy.

[5] In all fairness, this is not all old women, maybe not even most. However, most do seem to take their shopping very seriously. But once you are in the street again, it is all smiles and 'holas'.

rewarded with being attended when the moment came that I was the person who had been waiting the longest. I have now changed that philosophy with a new one; the squeaky wheel gets oiled... Much more useful and effective.

However, this alone, I have come to learn, is not enough. One must say it with conviction and belief that they will be served next regardless of the fact that it is not fair or just. An example: I was in the bread store. I was planning on making a special dinner for my husband's birthday and I wanted to get his favorite type of bread, *pan de payés*. I saw that there was only one loaf left. There was only one person in front of me and she opted for a baguette. I sighed in relief. While she was paying, I nervously scanned the street that passes the entrance and, to my horror, I saw an old woman moving quickly and purposefully over the cobblestone, with the help of her cane, angling for the bread store door. An eternity passed while the change was being given to the costumer in front of me. I broke into a sweat as I heard the strands of the summer beaded door being parted. I waited as long as I could and, before the baker even had time to make eye contact, I barked out, "*Medio kilo de pan de payés.*" It came out more like a question, a croak, a squeaking plea.

As the last croak of my pathetic order was dying away, the old woman said the same thing, but with a tone of voice and severity that suggested that, if this order was not completed, someone was going to get whacked by her cane. To my great frustration, the last half kilo of *pan de payés* of the day was awarded to her and not me. I stared mouth open and red faced as the old woman paid for what should have been my loaf of bread, tucked it into her wicker shopping basket and shuffled out. The baker looked at me as if nothing had transpired just moments ago and eagerly awaited my order now that I was the only person in the shop.

* * * *

Old men do not seem as hostile as the old women in the supermarkets. The elderly male population helps to keep everyone in tune with the slow but consistent pace of Menorca... about forty kilometers per hour. If it is not a tractor, sheep, cows, or pigs, it is an eighty-five to one hundred and thirty-year-old man on a scooter with yellow license plates. Observation suggests that this is the preferred mode of transportation of the older male population.

The yellow license plate is something that I find amazing and scary. The yellow license plate = no license needed to operate this vehicle. Scooters and little mini-cars fall into this category. I was told that vehicles that are made to go no faster than fifty kilometers per hour have this uniquely colored license plate. The reason that this yellow plate fills me with dread is because it begs the question: why do so many old men drive vehicles with this color plate? Is it because they were not able to renew their driver's license for reasons such as failing eyesight? Mental instability? Dangerously delayed reaction time? It amazes me that this idea does not occur to anyone else. I have never voiced this suspicion for fear that I will be labeled an evil American who would take away the rights of mobility of the geriatric community. I am also sure that it would be pointed out that, because Menorcans (and Europeans in general) are not sue-happy like us North Americans, such things do not need to be worried about. And, to be honest, I have not seen or heard of an accident being caused by a yellow-plated vehicle on Menorca.

* * * *

Many people have hypothesized as to why people live so long and healthily on the island of Menorca. Many say it is the Mediterranean air, while others say that it is the simple Mediterranean diet. Others suggest that it is the lack of stress that there was on the island before the tourist bang that started about twenty years ago. Still, there is little stress in Menorca compared to most places. Up until recently, Menorca was a world unto itself, protected from the fast pace and frantic lifestyle that one finds on the mainland in places like Barcelona and Madrid. Menorca is still protected in many ways. Fernando, when explaining Menorca to those who are unfamiliar with the place, describes it as 'a bubble, not popped by the real world'.

As with most things, I believe that the longevity found on the island has to do with a combination of all of the above. I know that I feel I am tapping into a life-prolonging serum when I breathe in the pure, salty air, eat and drink simple, conservative-free products and spend midday eating and relaxing with loved ones. I feel the years slip away when I spend the day covered in red mud on Cavalleria beach in the north, washing it off while watching the sun penetrate the warm, salty sea with me.

Maybe it is possible to live past one hundred, drug and pain free. The only thing I don't understand... why don't more people choose this way of life?

6

Gary the Seagull

"Oh, fly away, great bird so white…"
Richard Adams, Watership Down

Gary arrived one day, walking up the trail that starts at Santa Teresa, passes the Roman military fort, runs along the port of Sanitja and ends at the cliffs behind the lighthouse. My brother, Lane, was helping me that day in the museum and we were both outside sitting on the 200-year-old stone bench that curves out of the wall of the farm house enjoying the hot sun and the lull in customers. I saw from a distance a gray figure bobbing from side to side as it advanced up the trail towards us.

"It looks like a penguin."

"There are no penguins on the island, Lane, or in the northern hemisphere, for that matter."

He gave me an ironic grin and I knew what he was thinking… northern polar bears. My brother has astounded me for as long as I can remember with his plethora of trivial facts and information. To this day, I have never been able to figure out his sources. We were always together, lived on a remote farm, were in the same class, watched the same television programs and had the same friends, and internet did not yet exist, but he somehow gathered facts that I know were never presented to me. One day when we were very small, he taught me how to count to ten in Japanese and French. Another day, he proudly came up to me and recited all of the United States presidents in order of their presidency.

I remember on one spring day we had to stay inside because there had been a bear sighting on the ranch, which started a whole day of bear talk, my brother naturally being an expert on this topic. Of course, the first thing we talked about was what bears ate, starting with little blonde children like us. Our conversation wandered a bit and we began to ponder what polar bears ate. I had the great idea that polar bears must eat penguins (in my defense, I was around ten years old). My brother (one year younger than me) laughed and told me that it must be very difficult for polar bears since polar bears and penguins lived on opposite ends of the Earth. I, of course, did not believe him. I had seen cartoons with polar bears and penguins living together in a winter wonder land and, believing everything I see on TV, I naturally assumed that both lived in both of the poles. I remember saying something to the effect, much to the delight of my know-it-all brother, that, if that was true, then they would be called northern polar bears, not just polar bears. Many years later, I was telling Lane that I was going to see penguins in the south of Argentina while on vacation and that Fernando was trying to convince me to go even further south to see the glaciers of Antarctica. Lane had told me with a smile to watch out for polar bears.

"Well, what flightless birds do you have on the island then?"

"That would be injured birds. It looks like it's dragging its wings. Maybe it got hit by a car and has two broken wings."

"Or maybe it has the bird flu."

"Avian bird flu?"

"Isn't that a bit redundant, Lana? It's like saying K-9 dog flu."

By this point, the bird was on the patio and walking directly in front of us. It appeared to be a gray, mangy looking seagull. It walked to the far side of the patio and settled down next to the wall.

"If I had my gun, I would shoot it."

"Lane, you're horrible."

"But Lana, it looks like it is suffering and while it suffers it is going to give all of your customers bird flu."

"I seriously doubt that it has bird flu. I think that it is a seagull that has two broken wings and is very tired from walking in the hot sun."

"But it is too gray to be a seagull; seagulls are white, and it is not normal that it decided to sit down a meter from us. Conclusion, unidentified bird with bird flu that must be killed or chased off before it contaminates tourist."

"Maybe it's a Balearic shearwater."

"And that would be a gray, mangy, sick-looking type of bird?"

I ignored my brother's sarcasm. "It is a very protected bird that only breeds in the Balearic Islands. There are only something like 3,000 reproductive pairs in the world and they only have one chic per year and you want to kill it. The sign you walk past by the parking lot twice a day explains all about them and how privileged we are to have them here in the cliffs of Cavalleria. If you kill this bird, it might mean the extinction of the species."

"A little dramatic, no? Whatever it is, I think you should move it away from the bar where people are drinking and eating."

I agreed, not because of the danger it may pose to the tourists, but vice versa.

"I am going to get it some bread."

"Good idea; strengthen the bird flu within it."

"Paula will be back tomorrow; she can tell us what is wrong with it," I said over my shoulder as I went to get bread.

"Paula loves animals too much to be an objective veterinarian. She seems to lose touch with reality when it comes to animals... Remember when she swore that Manolo called her Mama? Granted, Manolo has some pretty strange meows, but Mama? And you both like animals more than people, so I would not be surprised if you cultivated the disease and intentionally gave it to the entire population so that all of Menorca could be a permanent wildlife refuge."

"Not a bad idea," I said as I tore some bread into little pieces. "Paula is a great veterinarian and I am sure that she will concur with my diagnosis of broken wings and not your bird flu theory."

I threw little bits of bread near to where the bird laid and it pecked at them listlessly.

"Maybe it is thirsty." I went into the storage room and found an empty five-liter jug, cut the top half off and filled the bottom half with water. As I walked out the door, a bit splashed over the edge and fell to the ground. Before I could take another step, the bird was up and running at me. The clear plastic confused it because, at first, it kept driving its beak wildly against it. I lowered it a bit and it stuck its head almost completely underwater. Once it figured out where the water was, it took deep gulps, throwing its head back after each swig.

While it was still drinking water out of the container in my hands, I said to my brother, "I guess I was right about it being thirsty. Do you think a bird with bird flu would drink so much so eagerly?"

"Animals with rabies drink lots of water."

"So now it has rabies? I will keep an eye out and let you know if it starts foaming at the beak."

After it greedily gulped down all of the water, it was more interested in the bread crumbs that I had scattered about. When it finished with what I had already sprinkled around, I began leading it crumb by crumb to the far corner of the terrace, to the pine trees and away from the museum and bar. The bird followed after me, wobbling side to side, dragging its wings on the ground until we reached a nice little area behind a stone wall with a soft carpet of pine needles in the shade. It settled down again near the wall and I left the remaining part of the bread beside it. I walked back to the museum, refilled the new bird trough, and brought it back and placed it beside the bread. It swiveled its head and watched me continuously, but did not move. "I think I will call you Gary," I said to the bird.

"Why would you give that sick bird such a stupid name?" my brother asked, having snuck up on us.

"Because the word for seagull in Spanish is *gaviota* so he is Gary la *gaviota*. And if I really think about it and give him (I had decided arbitrarily that it was male) a cool name, then he will not stick around. However, if I just give him a *whatever* kind of name, he will stick around and make me regret giving him a stupid name."

"There's some good logic for you. And to think that you graduated top of your class *and* Phi Beta Kappa. Apart from your amazing reasoning abilities, I thought he was a Balearic shearwater on the point of extinction, not a seagull."

"After looking at him for a while, I am pretty sure that he is a type of seagull, not a Balearic shearwater. But Fernando will be more likely to let me keep him here if he thinks he is a shearwater, so that's what we are going to tell him."

"Lying to your husband for the sake of a sick bird. Won't he notice the difference?"

"Roman pottery is the only thing that he can differentiate. Apart from that, he is like most men, oblivious to distinction... eye color, hair, plants, animals, etc.; I am sure you understand." I received a not-so-nice look, but continued, "It took him a year to distinguish Felipe, the all-white cat, from Manolo, the all-orange cat."

"Sounds like Uncle John."

This sent us both into peals of laughter, remembering the story that my aunt had just called and told us. My Aunt Anne will take care of anything that needs her to, even dirty stray cats that she is highly allergic to. She often asks my Uncle John to take the cats to the vet so that she does not have to be in a confined space with them. She spends about a half an hour before each vet trip explaining to my uncle the cat's name, how to remember the name (i.e. Patches for his black and white patches) and what exactly needs to be done to it at the vet. One day, Whiskers (named after his extremely long whiskers) looked really sick and my Uncle John was out working on the ranch, so my aunt decided that she would take him to the vet and suffer the consequences of being so near a cat for the twenty-minute car ride. She had no idea what could be wrong with the cat, so she asked the vet to look up Whiskers' file. There was no file for a cat named Whiskers. There were only files for 'cat'. Every time they had asked my uncle the name of the cat, he had replied 'cat'. Luckily, the receptionist at the clinic had labeled 'cat' as Cat #1, Cat # 2 and so on with a brief description of each cat, which was, luckily, very easy to decipher being that my aunt names each cat after its most distinguishing features with the futile intention of helping my uncle remember their names. I was counting on Fernando to have about the same amount of interest in birds.

As I was closing up the museum, Felipe, Manolo and Rey came to remind me that they wanted the leftover scraps of the day from the museum's bar.

"Lana, you know you are going to find only feathers tomorrow, don't you?" my brother asked on the ride home.

"Maybe not; these cats are pretty lazy." I knew Lane was most likely right and I tried not to be too hopeful.

Fernando had gone to the airport to pick up Paula, and I made dinner while we waited. When they arrived, I told Paula about the newest member of the Ecomuseum's team. Fernando and Paula listened as I explained about the *shearwater* and to Lane, who was trying to convince them that the bird should be killed the next day.

I prepared myself for a mound of feathers as we walked from the parking to the museum the next morning, but, to my surprise, Gary was settled down in front of the door of the museum with the three cats just as calm as they could all be waiting for their breakfast.

"This is the bird that you wanted to kill?" Paula accusingly asked Lane. "The reason that this bird is not flying and is gray and mangy looking is because it is a baby."

"Oops," my brother replied with a guilty grin on his face.

The first part of opening the museum is feeding the cats so that they don't bother us while we open. I took their food out past the edge of the terrace and into the forest (the opposite side to where I had left Gary the previous day) with the cats trotting along behind me. All part of our normal morning routine. I heard Paula laughing from the museum, turned to see why and saw that behind the three cats following me to the forest was Gary bobbing along, as well. I dumped out the cat food and started walking back. I called to Gary and rubbed my fingers together as if I had food, trying to get him to follow me away from the cats. He swiveled his head back and forth as if trying to decide the best course of action, cats or human, and then slowly started bobbing along behind me. I went into the museum and opened a can of tuna that we use to make *bocadillos* that we sell in the bar for the tourists. I came back out, can in hand, and threw a bit down on the tiled floor of the terrace. At first, he tried to eat it by pecking straight down. He must not have liked how the hard tile felt against his beak because he tried again angling his head sideways, parallel to the ground, and ate the rest of the tuna enthusiastically in this fashion. I lead him back to his side of the forest via tuna bits, where I hoped he would stay for the remainder of the day.

My hopes were dashed when I saw him appear five minutes later from behind the stone wall bobbing side to side back towards the museum.

"Shit, we will have to be watching all day to make sure that evil children don't chase him. I have no idea why this baby walked all the way from the cliffs to here and has decided to stay, but it is a safe bet that he has had a lot of stress and I don't want any out-of-control tourist adding to it."

Paula agreed with me on this and we were not looking forward to keeping the July crowds from bothering the bird.

I have to admit that, all in all, people behaved better than we thought they would. But why is it that the two jerks in the day are the only ones who you remember from the five hundred nice people? It is always the same. One asshole can ruin your entire day while a hundred nice people cannot make up for it. I never stay up late thinking about comments that I would like to make to all the nice people every day, or replaying their comments over and over in my head.

And so the first day with Gary went. He weaved between tables while most tourists took pictures of him and tossed him bits of food. I took his food to his corner about five times and made sure that his water was always full, but he always returned and wandered about the terrace. Only once on the first day did a child of about five years old start to run after him while his parents watched on unconcerned. I had prepared for this moment and was determined not to lose my cool. But, as I watched the parents watch the child chasing this terrified baby bird across the terrace, I lost it. I was out the door yelling at the kid to stop chasing the bird. The kid stopped, looked at me and then continued. I yelled again, not sure that the kid understood Spanish, so I just yelled 'NO' and 'NEIN' (covering 'no' in the languages that I could) a few times. The kid finally stopped, but that's when the parents started. They said to me (in Spanish), "He is only five; what's the big deal?"

I considered chasing them around the terrace with a knife to show them what the big deal was, but decided against it. I was just about to explain how it was a baby bird and that we were taking care of it, when I realized that, with these kinds of people, it did not matter. I was not going to waste my time explaining to them something they obviously could not comprehend. So, instead, I said, "We think that bird has the bird flu and we are waiting for someone to come pick it up and test it. If you want your kid to get near it, I am not going to take any responsibility."

Well, that got them into action. They picked their kid up so fast and he did not move from the table until they all left a few minutes later with me sending all the bad vibes I could after them.

Am I so different from others? Is it so strange that I do not want to harass other living things for my entertainment? My mom had always taught me that it was cruel to hurt or bother something else for my amusement. This included packing small begrudging dogs and cats around like babies, dressing animals up in clothing, chasing birds, scaring sleeping animals, etc. Why do people have to do these things? Why can't people enjoy seeing something else at ease and enjoy it too? Why do humans have the need to affect their surrounds? Why, why, why? It is something that frustrates me to no end.

By the end of the day, we had given Gary the entire contents of a kilo can of tuna (part went to pacify the cats so that they would not chase Gary off and eat his tuna).

"Fernando is going to kill us if he catches us feeding products of the bar to a bird."

Paula nodded in agreement and pointed out that processed canned food, preserved in olive oil, was probably not the best thing to be giving a baby bird anyway.

"Why don't you feed it grasshoppers," Lane jokingly said.

Paula and I looked at each other with *not a bad idea* looks on our faces and Paula headed out into the field. Gary bobbed along behind her and it was quite a sight, Paula with flip flop in hand ready to strike while baby seagull looks on.

After a few smacks with her flip flop, Paula had accumulated a handful of dead grasshoppers. She held one with legs still twitching out to Gary, who looked at it, pondered over what to do with it, then gingerly took it out of Paula's outstretched hand. He must have liked the crunch of the bug's body or the salty taste of grasshopper because he almost took Paula's fingers off while finishing the rest.

"How much can a seagull eat?" Lane asked.

"Apparently a lot. I think he thinks he needs more grasshoppers."

Gary was now taking a more active part in Paula's grasshopper hunting. Instead of just watching from a distance, he was now roaming the field alongside her.

Every time Paula would smack with her flip flop, Gary would beeline, running straight at her with beak open.

"This is not natural. The bird has webbed feet and it is being taught to hunt grasshoppers in a field. You and Paula are going to seriously mess up this bird."

We finished the day at the museum, giving the cats extra food in hopes that they would not eat Gary. On the way out to the parking lot, Lane had another feeding-Gary idea. "Aren't there tons of huge grasshoppers on the road every morning? If we run them over and collect the dead bodies, it would be easier than hunting them in the field with a flip flop."

We were impressed with this idea and Paula went back to the museum for a bag so that we would be ready to collect flattened grasshoppers in the morning. What Lane said was very true and we had commented many times how strange it was that so many huge grasshoppers were on the smaller roads in the morning. The only reason that I can think of why they do it is to try to escape the dew on the ground and plants in the morning. This phenomenon has almost caused me numerous car accidents, not because I try to miss the grasshoppers, but because the little finches in the area eat the flattened grasshoppers off the road and get so full that they can't take off as quickly as normal and appear to be stuck to the road by their bellies. I have had a few close ones swerving to avoid gluttonous birds and almost crashing into oncoming traffic.

The next morning, Lane, Paula and I piled into our Renault 4 and started off towards the museum. Once we were on the twisty country road that leads to the northernmost part of the island, we started looking out for concentrations of grasshoppers to run over. When we would come upon a patch of grasshoppers, Lane would swerve wildly, trying to run over as many as possible without running over the fattened little finches stuck to the ground. Once we had gone over a patch, Paula and I would jump out and collect the goods in a little paper bag from the museum's gift shop. The size of their flattened bodies amazed us and we began to wonder if they were locusts, not grasshoppers.

"Oh perfect," complained Lane. "Let the seven plagues begin: bird flu, locusts..."

Much to his disappointment, I pointed out that those were only two and that we were in Menorca, not Egypt.

By the time we got to the museum, we had filled the bag completely. "Wouldn't it suck if Gary isn't there after all this work we have done, scraping and pulling dead bodies off the road," commented my ever-optimistic brother.

To my relief, Gary was settled down in front of the museum door with the three cats, all waiting for their morning feeding. I fed the cats while Paula fed Gary the contents of the bag. Halfway through, Gary decided he was full of locust treats and wandered off. The day continued on as normal until a few hours later when we heard a violent 'o*stia puta*' from Fernando.

"Uh-oh," Paula said. "I think the boss found Gary's food bag."

After an hour-long lecture on sanitary practices and health inspections, Fernando calmed down and told us about how Gary had followed him and the students down at six in the morning to the military fort and watched them excavate for a while. "The students now call him Gary the Archaeologist."

The students, now feeling that Gary was one of them, invited him via bread crumbs over to where they were eating and let him join in. I went over to make sure that Lane had not told them that Gary had bird flu and found one of the students down on his hands and knees with a large piece of bread sticking out of his mouth. Much to the delight of the other students, Gary walked over and plucked the bread from his mouth. I was pretty sure that mouth-to-mouth feeding ruled out that Lane had shared his bird flu theory. When the student caught me looking at him still down on all fours, he gave me a sheepish grin... the same one that he gave me when I told him that I knew it was not water in his water bottle that he was adding to his soda in the alcohol-free student residence. I gave him a 'you are very weird' look, and left the students to feed Gary in any position that they chose. About half of the bread of the sandwiches went to the bird and I could see it coming... all of the bitching about how hungry they were before dinner.

When the students finished their break, they headed toward the museum to do lab work. Gary followed as far as the door and then decided that he maybe was not so interested in archaeology after all and continued roaming the terrace in the heat of the day while we continued working.

"Lana, for once your bird is doing something normal."

I followed Lane's gaze and saw Gary floating in the stone sink that we had converted into a bird bath/drinking trough a few years before.

The stone sink was the original sink of Santa Teresa. It is hand-carved local lime stone with the date 1872 carved on the front. It has two basins (like most modern sinks) with a drainage hole at the bottom of each. Fernando had found it disregarded and half buried against a stone wall near the corner of the house. We assumed that the original sink was thrown out when more modern, lighter and easier to clean sinks became readily available. He remembered it when we were planting new trees and putting gravel on the terrace after many of the pine trees fell over during brutal *tramontana* winds the winter before, leaving the terrace looking naked and forlorn. Fernando had bought along with the new pine trees a huge olive tree that most people date to be around 300 years old. We decided that the olive tree with its impressively gnarled truck should be placed in the center of the terraced ringed by little piece of *mares*, then by a border of larger rocks.

Fernando had decided on an olive tree for the centerpiece of the terrace, not just for its aged beauty, but also as a gift to the owner of Santa Teresa, Señor Olivar. Without Señor Olivar's faith in Fernando's project and love of archaeology, we would never have been able to create the museum and international archaeology field school that are now functioning better than we could have ever hoped for. Also, our contract was up that year and we thought a little ass-kissing might help with renovating it.

Fernando had the idea when he was looking through a book on Menorcan history and came across a part on the noble families of Menorca. He looked up the Olivar family and saw that in the center of their family's coat of arms was an olive tree. He happened to come across this around the same time that we were trying to decide what to do with the *tramontana* beaten terrace.

A tractor had to come to dig the holes for the trees and a crane set them in place. The hole for the olive tree was deeper than I am tall. Once the tree was settled in, they dumped huge sacks of *mares* around the trunk. Nicolas then put the rock border around the *mares* while the tractor and crane were helping the other trees into their new home. The tractor was about to leave when Fernando had the idea of placing the original stone sink in front of the olive tree to give the terrace a unique touch of history. I was worried that, if we put it in such a central place, someone would come and steal it, but, as we watched the small tractor strain under the sink's weight, I realized that it would not be moving again for a long time. Fernando was right; the sink gave the terrace a special touch.

I had asked Fernando if he cared if I stopped up the holes in the bottom and filled it with water so that the birds and cats could drink out if it. "Great idea. Just don't stop them up permanently in case someone in the future wants to use it for its original purpose. People are appreciating these works that were once considered cumbersome more and more and we don't want to alter something that is not ours."

I nodded patiently through Fernando's little monolog on how to treat historical patrimony and then set out to find what I could to not permanently stop up the holes. I scanned the bar for small circular objects and decided that a wine cork would be about the perfect size. Of course, there were none readily available and I had to wait for the two next corks from empty wine bottles in the bar. When I finally had them (not too long, thanks to my helping empty the wine bottles little by little into my glass when Fernando was not looking), I took them out to the stone sink and they fit perfectly into the stone holes. I dragged the hose over, filled it up and watched. At first, a bit of water escaped from one of the holes, so I jammed the corks in further. Once I was satisfied that it was water tight, I wandered back to the museum doorway and waited for the birds to come and refresh themselves.

The first week, there was not much drinking going on from any type of animal, but, by the start of the second week, word got around to the local fauna that there was fresh water to be had in the north. Finches and turtledoves became regulars and the cats figured out their new place to drink water. Luckily, the cats seemed completely unimpressed by the birds and the birds soon realized this and would come down to drink even when the cats were drinking or lounging in the shade of the olive tree.

In one of the stone sink basins was where Gary was now floating. He sometimes would splash about, bathing himself, but most of the day just floated. In the evening, Gary switched over from one stone basin to the other. While he was floating in the other side, Felipe went over to get a drink out of the unoccupied basin. He approached slowly and cautiously, put his two front paws on the side of the sink and lowered his head down to the water, his eyes never leaving the large bird floating beside him. He started to lap at the water with his little pink tongue and then jerked his head back as if he had been stung. He then turned away and walked back to the shade that the wall of the museum provides in the evening, plopped down and started to clean his fat belly. I had been watching this from the doorway of the museum and could not figure out Felipe's reaction. Gary had never moved or made a sound. Later on, Manolo did almost the exact same thing. I walked over to the sink to see what the problem was and saw it immediately. Gary had repeatedly shat in the sink while floating. I imagine that is why he had decided to changed sides.

I dragged the hose over and gently placed it into the shit-filled stone basin, trying not to scare Gary. When all of the bird crap had overflowed and only clean water remained, I turned off the hose, dragged it off the terrace and coiled it back up. Within minutes, Gary had switched to the other side, leaving another shit-filled basin.

Paula and I decided that we would take turns hosing the sink out a couple times a day. The cats did not really like it, but they adjusted and would come over to drink when they saw us with the hose. Gary passed the majority of the day floating in the stone sink and became the most frequently photographed thing in northern Menorca, followed by Felipe's 'four legs in the air, rigor-mortis' sleeping position, both rivaling the lighthouse, which had always received the most photos until the Ecomuseum weird animal zoo started.

Even Sonia, one of the best guides on the island, changed her speech of the area to her weekly group of British tourists to include Gary. "To the right of the port of Sanitja, you will see the oldest lighthouse on the island. To the left is a British defense tower built in 1800 during the British occupation of the island. Over here, floating in the antique stone sink, is Gary the seagull that the girls of the Ecomuseum are taking care of until he learns to fly."

Photos; photos; photos.

"I don't like that we are feeding Gary so many things that are not of a typical seagull diet," Paula commented one day while we were preparing a mix of leftover tuna and breadcrumbs for Gary's dinner. "What days do we have the fish market in Es Migjorn Gran?"

"Tuesdays, Thursdays and Saturdays," I answered without doubt, knowing because on those days I wake up a half an hour earlier to be the first one there when the doors of the supermarket open so that I have my select choice of fresh fish to prepare for dinner. "There are always some small fish like sardines we can pick up. I never buy them because I really don't know what one would do with them, but I don't think they will cost too much."

We had to wait two days until the next fish market and Gary sufficed on grasshoppers and canned tuna. When Tuesday arrived, we went to the supermarket where local fishermen rent a space three times a week and bought half a kilo of some fish that were a bit smaller than sardines for 2€ a kilo.

Gary was being a cat when we arrived and was waiting by the door of the museum with the others instead of floating. Paula opened the bag and tossed a fish to each one of the cats and then to Gary. Gary flipped the fish around a bit until its head was pointing into his beak, then swallowed it in one gulp. We tossed him another fish and he repeated the process, swallowing the fish head first. By the time we threw Gary his third fish, Rey (meaning King, named before she was tamed and before I knew her sex) had finished her fish and thought she was going to have a go at Gary's. She darted at Gary's fish, full of confidence until Gary opened his wings, made an enormous 'CA CA CA CA' sound and went running at her with a jabbing beak and flapping wings. Rey took off and did not come back the rest of the day while the rest of the startled cats looked at Gary with a new respect. Gary walked back to his fish, wings still spread and beak open, eyeing the cats with an expression that said, 'you think you're going to take my fish, do you'. I believe Gary was just as surprised as the cats with his impressive wingspan because, after he ate his fish, he kept his wings out and swiveled his head back and forth as if thinking, *well, well, what do we have here?*

After breakfast, Gary went to the sink, swished his beak back and forth in the water, presumably to clean it, and then just floated. It was work as normal until I heard Paula shriek my name. From the urgent tone of her voice, I was thinking plane about to crash into the museum, tsunami, armed and dangerous tourist, or something of the sort. I was not prepared for what actually came out of her mouth. "Lana, Lana look! Gary is doing yoga."

After the blood returned to my body, knowing now that I was not in mortal danger, I replied, "Yes, Paula, and Manolo called you Mama."

"Manolo *did* call me Mama and Gary *is* doing yoga. Look!"

I walked over to the window and saw that, indeed, Gary was doing yoga. He was on the side of the sink, on the flat stone surface with his left wing horizontally outstretched and his left leg also horizontally stretched below his wing. He held this position for a bit and then did the same with his right wing and leg. Once he was done with yoga, he went back to floating.

On Thursday when Paula went to get more fish for Gary, she told the girl running the fish stand that we were buying the fish for a baby seagull that we were taking care of. She loved the story and told Paula that she would save all of the fish guts for her if she wanted. Free fish guts are the kind of thing that excites Paula and she eagerly agreed.

As the days passed, Gary wandered around the terrace, floated in the sink and ate fish guts, but he showed no inclination of knowing that he should fly. The only time that he used his wings was to scare the cats or to do yoga. Paula came back from her day off and said, "We have a problem. I went near La Mola yesterday and saw a mommy seagull teaching a baby seagull that looked just like Gary how to fly. They were on a rock and she flew off in a circle and when she came back, they flew in a circle together coming back and landing on the rock. We can't teach Gary by example and I am worried after what I saw that he will not figure out how to fly in time to migrate."

"Do all seagulls migrate?" I wondered out loud. "This is a pretty temperate climate here."

We were not quite sure, so we looked Gary up on the internet. With keywords like seagull, gray beak, gray legs and Balearic Islands, we quickly found a picture of Gary, which we now knew was a *Larus fuscus*. For the first two years, they are a grayish white, and then their chest and belly become all white and their black beak and legs turn yellow. They come here to nest in spring, stay during the summer and then migrate in fall.

"Okay, so we have until fall to turn Gary into a fully functioning seagull. Any plans?"

Paula had the idea of baiting Gary up the lookout point in front of the museum that forms a ramp and then scaring him from behind so that he would (hopefully) fly off the edge of the ramp. I was not all for this idea because I hated the thought of scaring Gary, even if it was for his own good. Paula pointed out that we really did not want to make Gary too tame because it may hinder his natural instincts and cause problems when he returned to his natural habitat. But neither of us had the heart to scare Gary off the ramp, so we settled for holding fish high in the air so he had to flap his winds to get high enough to snatch the fish from our fingers. I think that this helped Gary understand the functionality of his wings because he started bouncing around the terrace, flapping his wings and getting about a meter off the ground each time.

After about a week of bouncing, I heard Paula shriek my name, which I now knew meant an animal-related event and not mortal danger. "Lana, Lana, Gary is flying!"

I followed her gaze and saw Gary next to the large brush pile where the field in front meets the pine trees behind the terrace, about twenty meters from the museum door.

"He flew from his sink to all the way over there. He did not get very far off the ground... but he was flying!"

Gary's days became divided between ground-skimming flying and floating in the sink. Each day, he was able to fly a little farther and a little higher until he was easily clearing the tops of the pine trees, circling back and landing on the roof of the museum. He was not as graceful as other seagulls that we had observed. He flew with his legs spread out to the sides instead of neatly tucked under and kind of wobbled side to side. His landings were so rough that they looked almost painful, but Paula and I watched on like the proud mommies we were.

Now, when evil children chased after him, he would take off, circle back and land on the roof, always on the northern most point overlooking the port and the evil children who gazed up at him in frustration.

I think his flying helped him to understand that he was not a cat and he began to wait for his morning fish up on the roof while the cats loitered in front of the museum door. I loved showing up in the morning and seeing on the roof of Santa Teresa the red happy fish weather vane to the south and Gary to the north. As soon as he saw one of us come out of the museum door with the fish bag, he would swoop down from the roof and land next to the cats, waiting for his breakfast. He began to take longer flights and would only show up for his feeding times, in the morning, around four in the afternoon and then once more around seven before we left. "Our baby is growing up," Paula said as she wiped an imaginary tear (that was pretty close to not being imaginary) from her eye.

He became more and more hesitant to fly down for his fish guts, especially if there were people around. Paula started whistling for him, trying unsuccessfully to imitate the sound of a seagull, every time she brought fish out so that he would associate the food with the whistle and come down less hesitantly. It worked at first with Gary, but worked all too well with the cats. Every time Paula whistled, the cats would jump up from the naps in either the forest or the tile floor of the museum and come running at her meowing, answering her whistle announcing fish. It caused much amusement among tourists when Paula whistled and Gary would flap down and all the cats would charge at her, fur and feathers surrounding her all with the common goal of eating fresh fish guts.

Gary started to only show up once a day and, in late September, stopped showing up altogether. The first day that he did not show up, Paula was traumatized. "He's going to be so hungry. I hope he knows how to fish better than he flies."

I sadly laughed, picturing Gary's distinctive, wobbly flying style.

"I am sure he does, Paula," I said, trying to comfort her. "It is better that he gets practice while the weather is still good."

Gary did not show up the next day, either. "Hey, Paula," Lane said, "I watched a documentary once that said seagulls have a memory span of two days, so I hate to inform you that, if Gary does not show up by the end of the day, he will not remember the Ecomuseum or us and, therefore, will never come back."

My brother is very good at teasing with a straight face, but I can always tell when he is fibbing, but most cannot, so I quickly added, "Lane, that is such bullshit and you know it. Birds have the same migratory patterns all of their lives and I have even heard that some birds have one mate for life, so knock it off, you shit."

He gave his wicked grin, knowing that I had caught him in a lie, but Paula was still upset. "You know, Paula, it is around the time that his species migrate. Maybe we did better than we thought as mommy seagulls and he is doing exactly what he is supposed to be doing."

"Fat chance. That bird's got no hope."

"Well, our mom did everything right and look how you turned out," I snapped.

We continued to search the skies and, every time a shadow flew over the gravel, we would run out and check. But no Gary. Paula and I consoled ourselves in the fact that we did the best that we possibly could. The leaves began to turn colors and fall from the trees on the terrace and we closed the museum during the last week of October as usual. As Paula and I dragged all the tables and chairs in to be stored in the museum for winter, we reminisced about the year. Gary was without a doubt the highlight of summer.

*　*　*　*

I reopened up the museum in April for *Semana Santa*. We get many tourists from the mainland during holy week and it is usually worth opening up for. I was by myself, so the work seemed double. To top it off, it is almost always about ninety percent super Catalan people who take their nationalism so far that they will not speak to you in Spanish even if they know that you cannot understand Catalan and that you both have Spanish as a common language. I did my best and listened to many lectures about how I needed to learn Catalan if I continued to stay in Catalonia. I bit my tongue and never once pointed out that the Balearic Islands are not part of Catalonia, even if many Catalan people would like to think so. I get most irritated by these lectures because I know they are part right. I should make a more of an effort to learn Catalan and especially the dialect of Catalan that they speak here on the island, Menorquín.

I survived *Semana Santa* and felt like a train had run over me. I was looking forward to the coming month and to nice British tourists who envy me for my Spanish (never looking down on me because I don't speak Catalan, albeit many, like most tourists, not knowing that the language Catalan exists).

On April 22, I had a surprising amount of people for that early in the season. The weather was unseasonably pleasant and I think everyone took advantage of the nice day and decided to drive around and have a drink on any outside terrace they could find open. I noticed that many people seated on the terrace were pointing, laughing and taking pictures. The bar blocked my view of the ground, so I could not see what the people were gawking at.

I asked a tourist at the bar who was about to order, "Is it a big white cat in a strange pose that everyone is looking at?"

"No," he replied. "Actually, it is a big white bird."

I dashed out the door and there was Gary, weaving in and out of the tables. He looked exactly the same, still a scraggly gray. I told the tourists at the bar that he had to wait because my baby bird that I had raised last year had just arrived from his migratory flight and must be famished. I rushed in, opened a can of tuna, took it out and dumped its contents onto the flat part of the stone sink. Gary angled his head sideways and ate all the tuna in a few gulps. He swished his beak, then took a few deep swigs of water and proceeded to float. I dealt with the customer who was laughing at my excitement over a seagull, and then grabbed the phone and called my mom. It was about 2 am in California, but I was too excited to care. I yelled, "Mom, Mom, guess who just showed up at the museum?"

She groggily told me that she had no idea and, when I yelled 'Gary', she said, "Oh my God, you woke me up for that?"

But I could tell that she was grinning. I called Fernando and he laughed and said he could not believe it. Gary did some yoga and floated almost all of the day. I fed him more tuna and then he was off, deciding that he had other things to do. That night, I sent an email to Paula telling her what good seagull mommies we were.

Paula started work a few weeks later and we started with the fish gut routine again. Gary came at least once a day, usually around four or five pm when there was a lull in customers. One day, Paula had finished her distribution between cats and bird of fish guts and Gary walked up the lookout point and flew from there. As he took off, I noticed a feather fall from his wing into the field. Even though I had seen it fall, I thought I would never find it among the stickers. But I walked to where I thought it had fallen and there it was. I came back with my trophy and showed it to Paula. I could tell how much she wanted it, so, after a few seconds of selfish greed, I gave it to her. After all, she was the mommy who had killed the most grasshoppers and picked up the fish guts three times a week. She almost cried when I did and, as far as I know, she still has Gary's feather kept amongst her most precious things.

In August, more and more people started showing up and there was no time when the terrace was empty. Gary would sit up on the roof, but would not come down and, around mid-August, he stopped coming altogether. But this time we were happy. Our worst fears had not come true. Our baby seemed to be a perfectly functioning seagull.

* * * *

The next year, I had April 22 marked on my calendar, but Gary did not show up. All of our repeat customers knew about Gary and that he had returned, and each one asked if he had shown up for a third year straight. At first, I answered, 'not yet', but, as June rolled around, I started answering with a brave smile, "No, but hopefully he has a girlfriend and is doing seagull things."

A friend who came and stayed a few days in June had given me a book to read that she had enjoyed as a child and even more so as an adult called *Watership Down* by Richard Adams. I still had a few hours free a day and started to read it. I was struck with nostalgia when I got to a chapter called Keharr. It was about an injured seagull that the rabbits (the main characters) had helped and then befriended. It made me long for Gary. I thought, Keharr (meaning big water in the language seagulls speak, according to the book), what a cool name that would have made for Gary. I remembered back to his first day at the museum when Lane had teased me about the name I had given him.

Around this time, I had been toying with the idea of writing down all of my adventures in Menorca. I decided then, being inspired by the chapter Keharr, that I would begin with a chapter on Gary, and started writing.

I was still reading the chapter of Keharr (almost finished, truly appreciating now how great Keharr was) and writing about Gary when some of my friends came to the museum with a bottle of wine so that we could enjoy the terrace and relax a bit before the real tourist season started. It was June 21 and the Sant Joan festivals, the real start of tourist season, were about to start. We would not have another time to chat and relax until late September. We were munching away on anchovy stuffed olives and drinking a good Pinot Noir that they had picked up while driving around the countryside of France when one of my friends jokingly asked, "So, is that Gary?"

I thought he was teasing because I had told them about Gary, even though they had never seen him and also (in my intoxicated state) told them about Keharr in the book I was reading and the chapter I was currently trying to write. I turned anyway, knowing that I would be laughed at, but no, there was Gary on the terrace. He had just flapped down from the roof, but I had not seen him because my back was to him and the ocean, so that my friends could enjoy the view. I could not believe it. His chest was much whiter, which I had been expecting, but, apart from that, he was the same old Gary. I jumped up and opened the good old can of tuna, and he ate greedily. When he was full, he walked up the lookout point and flew off. We toasted to the third year of Gary and finished our wine.

Paula was starting work in a week and I called to tell her the great news. The next morning, I went and bought fish, not fish guts, to celebrate Gary's return. Gary came in late that afternoon and landed on the roof. When I whistled for him to come down, all of the cats came charging out of the forest. Just like the good old days. After a few weeks, there were more and more people on the terrace. One day,

Miguel, the newly tamed black cat, decided that, after eating his fish, he was going to try to pounce on Gary. Bad idea. Miguel pounced; I yelled; Miguel looked at me while in mid air and did not see that Gary had outstretched his wings, prepared his beak and was ready for him. Miguel turned, looked, startled and luckily fell short of Gary. I do not think that Gary was too impressed with either all the people or the new black cat that wanted to eat him and, soon after, he stopped coming.

It is still summer and sometimes I see him perched upon the roof, but he has decided for now that he is a self-sufficient bird. But I always have a can of tuna ready, just in case.

Note: While finishing up the other chapters of this book, Gary returned on May 30th, 2009, marking his fourth consecutive year of returning home to visit his mommies.

7

What's a Yank Doing Here?

Being a foreigner living in a new country means you give up your right to privacy in the eyes of most people. Everyone wants to know everything about you; how you got here, why you are here, what you are doing, what do you think about the place, the food, the people, etc. An accent seems to wipe out people's inhibitions and oftentimes their manners, asking questions that they would never ask a stranger of their own culture.

Most people are sincere and well intentioned, and honestly do not consider that working with the public means that I have to answer these questions about fifty times a day. When people are kind, I don't mind answering them and give them a quick summary that usually makes them smile. But when, for example, certain British tourists ask in a condescending, know-it-all fashion, 'so what's a Yank doing here', I reply, "I am Spanish, but I had a nanny from the States, hence the 'Yank' accent when I speak your language."

In my work as course coordinator of the archaeology field school, I have various documents prepared that answer frequently asked questions. I just cut and paste, or attach the pre-readied answer. I thought about typing up and printing out a document explaining how I got here, why I am here and all the typical questions that I am asked throughout the day and hand it out to those asking. But, I vetoed the idea because I could see where some might view it as rude.

*   *   *   *

Winter can be very depressing on Menorca. The *tramontana* wind blows and blows, howling against the windows and banging the green shutters of every home. Even the most balanced person becomes edgy. Many locals wander around in a red-eyed daze when the *tramontana* blows for more than three days straight. Menorca has the highest rate of suicides in all of Spain and many locals account this to the wind, saying the wind makes people do strange things.

Fernando had recently ended a ten-year relationship and was not too enthusiastic about spending the winter alone, battling against the wind and scraping salt off his windshield. Luckily for him, the oil tanker *Prestige* went down and created the worst oil spill since Exxon. Instead of playing the odds of the *tramontana* wind, Fernando decided to pack his bags and help clean up the oil spill in Galicia.

I was studying abroad in Córdoba, Spain when the oil tanker went down. I had two weeks after my program ended before my return flight. I was not too pleased with myself. I had gotten too drunk too many times and had had very un-student-like relations with my Spanish professor. I felt that I had done what the typical 'American' does in Spain and felt ashamed. I remembered my aunt telling me not to be an 'ugly American' when abroad, and that was exactly what I felt like. I wanted to redeem myself. I had watched the news nightly with my wonderful host family and knew all about the volunteers cleaning up the oil spill.

So I booked a train to La Coruña. I went there because the man at the ticket counter told me that was the best place to go for cleaning up the oil spill. My host family waited with me until my train pulled out of the station, waving until they became little dots on the horizon.

After various delays, I arrived at La Coruña around midnight in the middle of a downpour. I was busy cursing myself and my stupid ideas when an old woman with an umbrella walked up to me and asked me if I needed a place to stay. I loved her instantly for the fact that she looked at me and my beat-up backpack, cursing myself as if this was the most normal thing in the world one does when one is in need of a place to stay in the middle of the night in a downpour. She told me she had a pension not too far away for 12€ per night.

As we walked back to her pension, I asked if she knew anything about how to be a volunteer cleaning up the oil spill. She told me that she thought that I would need to be part of an organized team (something that I already knew, tried to do, could not, and, therefore, tried to forget). But, there was a Spanish couple around my age in her pension that was on their way to clean up the oil spill in the morning and that I should talk with them. So I did. They seemed very nice and I liked them instantly; Miriam and Marcos. They told me that they were on their way to a small town called Carnota where they were signed up as volunteers. I asked if I could tag along in case there was an opening in Carnota. They said 'sure', and we grabbed a bus together.

Carnota was in chaos. This very small, coastal town was being invaded by well-intentioned volunteers and people who wanted to take their pictures and say that they helped clean up the oil spill. The list that my new friends had signed up on was nowhere to be found. We walked into the city hall to see if we could get some advice. A slightly hysterical-looking man was on the phone. He looked at us and asked me where I was from.

"California."

"We even have people here from California!" he screamed into the phone. "We cannot deal with your group! Go clean up oil somewhere else!" He slammed the phone down, looked us over and barked, "What!"

"We came to help clean up the oils spill," my new friend, Miriam, meekly said.

"Are you part of a team?"

"We registered as volunteers a while ago and were told to come here today, but no one can find the list that we are supposed to be on."

I did not point out the fact that this did not pertain to me. My plan was just to let him assume that all three of us were on the list.

"Well, if there is no list, I cannot help you. Now, if you will excuse me, I have a lot of work to do."

There was only one bus per day in and out of Carnota and it had already dumped us off and left. We were all in the same position... screwed. The schoolhouse was full of volunteers from Menorca, the gym was full of volunteers from Sevilla, and the only hotel was just full. As we left the town hall with this bad news, it started to rain hard. We decided to do the only logical thing that people could do in this situation: find a bar and get drunk.

After five minutes of walking in the rain, we found a bar and started on our journey of getting drunk, talking louder and louder about our misfortune when the owner came over and told us that he had a house in construction and he would be happy to let us camp there if we wanted to. The house had no floor, no windows, some walls, no doors, no electricity and no running water. But it had a roof and it was raining. The owner of the bar was kind enough to hang a light bulb via a very long extension cord so that we could see our new dwelling.

Because I had been staying with a host family, I did not have a sleeping bag with me. My two new friends did, however. We zipped the two sleeping bags together and I jumped in the sack with these Spaniards who I had met that day. The situation worked out well because, otherwise, we most likely would have died of hypothermia in separate sacks, and me for sure with no sack.

In the morning, we headed down to the plaza in front of town hall in hopes that some team would pick up three extras. After being jumbled around a bit, we heard a rumor that Menorca was taking in strays.

I found out later that the Menorca group never showed up except for one dedicated volunteer. Their original destination was a small island off the coast of Galicia. The weather was very bad and no boats would take them out. Fernando told the others that he would go and scout out another work location further north. He arrived just before the tsunami of well-intentioned volunteers in Carnota and was able to get housing for his group in the local schoolhouse and three meals per day. He called the group to share the good news. The Menorca group had, by this time, settled down, finding a nice bar, and informed Fernando that they were fine where they were and would wait for the bad weather to clear. Fernando wanted to clean oil. The only thing he needed now was a *Menorca group*.

We saw a short, hairy Spaniard standing on a cement bank so that he was above the crowd. We could not hear what he was saying, so we squirmed through the crowd to get closer. It appeared that he was trying to organize a haphazard group of people. When he saw us approaching, he asked, "Do you have a group?"

All three of us shook our heads and Fernando deemed us Menorcans. I had no idea where Menorca was at the time, but I was happy I could clean up oil.

We were directed to get geared up in a large warehouse-like building. We were given various items and shown how to put them on. There was a full body jumper, which we pushed into our rubber boots. I wear a size 37 in Spain and was give a pair of size 42 rubber boots. It was as close as we could get. The ends of my sleeves were duck tapped around my wrists and gloves were slipped on and went well past the duck tape. A painter's mask was draped around my neck and we were set. I was almost out the door when Miriam stopped me. "One more thing." She wrote something on my back in big black marker. I was now 'Californiacation'.

We were herded onto a bus, given a sandwich, which we were told to eat before we got there, and preceded on our way to what we would all later call 'our beach'. I had seen, on the news, people picking up little balls of oil and scrubbing rocks with toothbrushes. Our beach was nothing like that. It had carpets of oil. Fernando organized us into pairs and Miriam and I paired up. We had to get the oil from the beach to the large container that a truck would come and pick up later. The container was about a ten-minute walk from the beach if you were unburdened. We formed a double chain, each pair about ten meters from the other. When a rubber bucket was passed to you, you had to run-walk with your partner to the next pair, pass the bucket and then hurry back to your position to receive the next bucket. We rotated as geese do when flying south for the winter so that the ones in the front would do the hard work for a while and then fall to the back when tired.

When it was our turn to collect oil from the beach, I stared unbelieving at the amount of oil that we had not even made a dent in all day long, until Miriam nudged me and we began filling buckets. The oil rolled up like a rug, which made it relatively easy to fill rubber buckets quickly. After about a half an hour, I began to feel dizzy from the toxins that were so overpowering that my mask could not keep them out. Just when I thought I was going to faint, it was our turn to fall to the back.

Now that my gloved hands were completely covered in oil and I could not touch myself anywhere, I realized that I itched everywhere. I had no way to tackle the problem and I was overwhelmed by relief and almost cried at the beautiful insight of others when a woman came up to us and said, "Hi, I'm *manos limpias*, clean hands. Is there anything I can do for you?"

I was embarrassed to ask her to scratch my face. When she saw me hesitate, she said, "Don't hold back; I have blown about twenty noses and even scratched someone's ass. It is what I am here for."

She scratched my entire face and poured water into my mouth from a squeeze bottle. There was not much she could do about my need to go to the bathroom because that would mean cutting my jumper off, so I just held it.

When the day was declared done, we took turns cutting each other's jumpers off with an X-Acto knife. There was a bottle of olive oil next to the X-Acto knife and I had no idea what it was for and even less so when I saw someone slathering it on his arms. I asked Miriam, but she had no idea either. After watching three people, a pattern emerged; people with petrol on their skin where using the olive oil and the petrol amazingly came right off.

I was so tired that I fell asleep on the short bus ride back. When we got back, Miriam and I decided to sneak into the gym where the Sevilla group was staying and use their showers. Marcos said that he would meet us back at where we were staying. There was no problem in using the showers. There were so many people our age that no one even gave us a second glance. The water was freezing and the thought of going back and sleeping in a cold construction site was not the most appealing. While in the showers, we saw a girl scrubbing a spot on her arm absolutely raw and shared our olive oil secret. After this passing on of information, we toweled off our shivering bodies, dressed and hiked home.

We found Marcos with a two-liter bottle of cola, a cheap bottle of wine and three plastic cups.

"Woohoo, *calimocho* time!" Miriam excitedly said.

"I hope that that word does not mean cola mixed with red wine."

"It is soooo good. Don't talk bad about it until you try it."

Marcos mixed half and half and we made a toast to our first day of cleaning up *chapapote*.

It was not great, but it was not as bad as I thought it would be. After two glasses, I asked, "What the hell is *chapapote*?"

They both burst out laughing and Miriam mockingly explained, "It is all that black stuff that we have been cleaning up all day long."

"You mean *petróleo*?" I mocked back.

"Oh please, Lana. That is the technical word. *Chapapote* is a much more fun word for all that black shit."

When we finished both bottles, we slipped into the sack. We were grateful that Marcos had gone out for *calimocho* supplies, but would have preferred that he used the time to shower as we had done. Even so, we were all out in less than five minutes.

We woke up with frozen noses. Galicia can be brutally cold in the winter. The cold was humid and it entered our already sore bones from sleeping on the ground for two days. Miriam and I were both dreading going to the bathroom, which we both had to do badly. We sucked it up, walked out of our shelter into the freezing wind, pulled our pants down, squatted and tried to pee while our bare asses froze off. It was so cold that neither of us could go, even though we both needed to desperately. Miriam decided that small talk would help. "This is sure one way to wake your ass up in the morning."

I chuckled at her comment and then we both started to shake with laughter as steam from our warm pee surrounded us.

"Yes," I agreed. "A perfect way to start off a day of cleaning *calimocho*," I said, proud to use my new vocabulary word.

Miriam laughed so hard that she lost her balance in her squatting position and fell in the puddle of her own pee. She stayed sitting that way, unable to do anything else, until her fit of laughter subsided. When she could finally breathe again, she said, "It's *chapapote*. *Chapapote* we are going to clean. *Calimocho* is what we drank last night."

To this day, I cannot get the two words straight.

We were suiting up when Fernando came over to where we were and told Miriam and I that we were going to be *manos limpias* today. My sore body cheered. I would much rather blow noses and scratch asses than sling heavy buckets of oil.

It was a difficult day to be *manos limpias* because it rained the entire day, a freezing, pelting kind of rain that put everyone in a bad mood. People found it hard to breathe through the wet cheap masks and we spent the day running up and down the rows pulling off and putting on people's masks. The choices were die of lack of oxygen or die of toxic overdose. Snot was as abundant as the oil and everyone itched where the rain tricked into their jumpers. People who had their masks off for more than an hour started to get nose bleeds, and Miriam and I had to cover that, as well. Miriam was a nurse and had no problem, but I was not accustomed to cranky, bleeding people.

During the last hour or two of work, a van showed up and a media crew got out with two people dressed for cleaning oil. On the right breast of their jumpers was a PP logo. I had no idea what it meant until Miriam explained later that it was the symbol of the right-wing political party in Spain. "The People's Party," she said with sarcasm.

They came over and plunked next to the people putting oil in a bucket. At first, they seemed more interested in streaking their own jumpers with oil than with cleaning it up. After five minutes of decorating themselves with oil, they looked like we did after an entire day. They then began to help roll it up and put it in the bucket with the cameras clicking away.

After twenty minutes of constant filming, Fernando came storming up to them and told them that this was 'our beach' and that they had no right using us in their farce. Angry words were exchanged and they finally left. I was surprised when Fernando threw a ball of *chapapote* after them. No one else seemed to be surprised, because they all cheered and threw their own balls.

Miriam explained that a lot of people blamed the PP for the extent of the damage because the president, who is of the PP, could have done many different things to help contain the oil spill when the first maydays were received. But he did not. His inaction caused the spill to contaminate all of Galicia, the main fishing industry of Spain, and parts of the south of France instead of a sole isolated harbor, for example. "I can imagine today's pictures will be titled something like, 'the PP cares' or 'we made a mistake, but we are helping to set it right'. Assholes."

Miriam and I decided to skip a freezing shower in exchange for showing our gratitude to the man who was providing us with free housing. Translation, we decided to go drink beer and play darts. It was then that I realized it was their last night here. They had to be up in the morning to catch the bus out.

Being that they would be taking my bed with them, I decided to accompany them to the bus stop in the morning. We exchanged emails, gave sincere hugs, and then my new friends were gone. Leaden down with my backpack, I did not really know what I was going to do. I walked to the only bar open that early in the morning and ordered an espresso. Five minutes later, Fernando and a few of his followers came in for coffee. I smiled and asked Fernando what time we were going to start work.

"You are part of my team?"

I assured him that I was and had been for the last two days.

"Then why are you not staying with us in the schoolhouse?"

"Because someone who was staying there said there was no room." I explained my last two days and the fact that my friends and bed had left.

He told me not to worry, Manu would see to everything I needed. Manu smiled at me and I knew that everything was going to be okay. Manu seemed to be Fernando's right-hand man in the oil cleaning operation, and appeared to be competent and kind.

Manu somehow produced extra blankets for me and found a space on the floor between Fernando and himself. I could tell that Manu had a crush on Fernando and felt honored that he gave me a space that was so special to him (I later found out that Fernando, for whatever reason, attracts homosexual men like honeybees to pollen). I stashed my bag and went out to gear up. Now that Miriam and Marcos were gone, Manu helped to gear me up. He even wrote 'Californiacation' on the back of my jumper. At least he knew that I had been working with Menorca, even if Fernando did not.

The bus driver was instructed by officials to take us to a different place and, when we arrived, it was obvious that we would not be able to work there. The waves broke against the cliff sides and there was no way to get at the oil. In our group was a man from Galicia[6] and he said that, if we walked along the coast, 'our beach' was only about a two-kilometer hike. Everyone agreed to the trek and we started off. I quickly fell behind, trying not to lose with each step my rubber boots that were five sizes too large.

I figured that the others had reached 'our beach', but did not understand why they just stood at the top of the hill staring. I knew they were not waiting for me because no one looked back to where I was struggling along. When I finally reach the group, no one had moved yet and I asked from behind, "What's going on?"

No one answered me and, as I topped the hill, no answer was needed. I stood stunned with the rest of the group. On 'our beach' was the biggest mammal I had ever seen. Dead. A bloated black tongue stuck out from the whale's mouth and there was no doubt as to what had killed it.

As I stared, unable to move, I felt something on my face and realized that was I crying copiously. I was embarrassed and went to turn my face when I realized that every other face in our group was equally streaked with tears. We stayed stunned and crying for a few minutes until one of our group members, I don't remember who, moved towards the majestic creature. The movement broke our

---

[6] This may seem normal; however, further from the norm it could not be. The government paid all of the fishermen in Galicia for their loss of work. Many Galicians bragged that they were making more drinking in the bars than they ever had fishing. It was very disheartening to see as a volunteer.

spell and we all followed down to the beach. I had been so overwhelmed by the whale that I had failed to notice the military on 'our beach'. There were easily over fifty men. Some of our group members started taking photos and making phone calls. I had my camera, but felt that I would somehow be violating this magnificent being by taking pictures of its unnatural death.

I could not take my eyes off the huge black tongue that protruded from the whale. Someone was shaking my shoulder and, when I turned, I saw an angry face in a camouflage jumper. "You can't be here; this is a restricted area."

"Why?" the Galician asked, still crying, "Do you not want anyone to see what your precious government has done, you fascist asshole?"[7]

"*Our* government did not do anything. It was the fault of a stupid captain and *una mierda de* oil tanker. You all need to leave here."

"We have been cleaning this beach and will continue to clean it whether you are here or not. We have already called the press so that everyone can see the impact of the oil spill. This incredible creature's death will not be in vain and will not be covered up. The press should be here within a few minutes. I don't think it would look good for you to try to remove us by force." This was Fernando speaking. He was a much less physically imposing figure then any of the military men, but had an air about him that made people think twice about messing with him.

---

[7] Up until recently, two years of military service for males were mandatory in Spain, which many people resented. Many Spaniards thought that anyone who elected to do more military service was a fascist or at least right-wing thinking. It did not help at the moment that many Spaniards were blaming the current President of Spain, part of the PP, right-wing party, for the extent of the oil spill.

The military man decided against trying to remove us by force in front of the press, and turned his back to us and walked to where the others in camouflage were. They organized, made a chain, and started hauling oil from the beach. We formed a chain, much more scraggily, parallel to them, and started the day's work. The press came and took pictures of the whale and it was on the news that night.

The next few days that followed were similar until New Years Eve. Before midnight, the press came and wanted to film volunteers celebrating. Fernando did not want the image of volunteers to be drunken, out of control pot-smokers, which was pretty much the scene in the schoolhouse at the moment. He also did not think it would be good for the kids of the town to see what was going on in their classroom while they were on vacation. So Fernando barred the press from coming in and anyone who wanted to talk with them had to go outside. The press was not happy, but they took what they could get.

Meanwhile, the Galician of the group was scrounging up a celebratory dinner. He came back with a load of prawns as a starter to our pasta. We pushed all the tables we could find together and had a nice long table where we could all sit together. During the course of the dinner, someone set a ball of tin-foil next to me and everyone else. I opened the foil and found twelve grapes. I thought it was a strange way to present dessert and my perplexed face caught Fernando's attention. He explained that it was tradition in Spain to eat a grape with each bong of the clock that marked the hour. Each grape swallowed with the corresponding bong represented a wish for the coming New Year.

When the hour neared, people climbed up on the chairs and started clapping their hands, egging on the midnight hour. I was not sure why or how everyone agreed that this was the correct thing to do, but it felt right, so I joined as well. When the hour finally arrived and the old year became the new, everyone gave a short cheer and started swallowing grapes. Eating twelve grapes in time with the twelve bongs of the clock is not an easy thing to do and I gave up at around number eight. After everyone finished their grapes, we all cheered and applauded. Then people started making circles around the table, hugging and double kissing all on both cheeks.

After a bit of clean up, it was decided that everyone with cars was now in charge of taking us all to the neighboring town that had a much better nightlife than small Carnota. There was no room for me and I volunteered to sit on Fernando's lap, which he did not object to. When we arrived, everyone attacked the bars except for Fernando and me. We decided on a leisurely walk in the moonlight along the oil scum and sand. We talked about many things and I appreciated that he spoke clearly and slowly so that I could keep up with his Spanish.

When we were back on the dock, I suddenly found my back pressed up against a wall and Fernando kissing me passionately. I had not expected such a stealthy and passionate act from serious Fernando, but welcomed it completely.

I had to leave the next day to catch my plane, and, in order to do that, I had to catch the 6 am bus out of Carnota. Fernando and I had talked all night and each drove cars full of very drunk volunteers, including the original drivers and owners of the cars, back to the schoolhouse. Fernando waited with me at the bus stop and, by 7:15 am, it was clear to both of us that no bus was coming.

"This is not uncommon on New Year's Day," Fernando told me. "But don't worry; I will get you to where you need to go."

I had no idea how he planned to do this, but had seen him in action during the last week and had no doubt.

He came running back five minutes later with keys in his hand. "Let's go."

"He gave you permission to take his car?" I asked, referring to one of the original drivers the night before.

"Not exactly, but it takes an hour to get to La Coruña where your train is and an hour to get back. I doubt that he will be awake by then. If he does wake up, he will be happy that he is in one piece and still has a car when I finally get back, which would not be the case if I had not driven it back from the bars... so don't worry."

We tore off in direction of my waiting train and made it just in time to exchange emails and a final kiss. I boarded the train and was homeward bound.

We emailed and spoke on the phone continuously throughout my last year of college. He came out to visit me once and I went to Menorca for the first time during my spring break (after finding out where it was).

Fernando was in conqueror mode and the two weeks were full of picnics, hikes along the coast, breakfast in bed and romantic dinners. I fell in love with Fernando and the island. He asked if I was interested in coming for the summer. I told him that I had to work during the summer because I still had to complete a fall semester in order to graduate and I had to pay housing, car insurance, etc., in Santa Cruz, which was one of the most expensive places to live in California, if not the entire USA. He asked if I would be interested in working the summer in his museum. He desperately needed an English-speaking receptionist for the vast amounts of British tourists who came to the museum daily. It was a perfect solution.

After an entire summer of working together, neither of us had any doubts. We wanted to spend the rest of our lives together. After I graduated, I married Fernando, moved to Menorca and have had many adventures, but never any regrets.

8

Just When You Think It's Over... It Starts Again

Almost every time a Spaniard discovers my nationality, the conversation takes a pointed turn starting off always with 'AMERICANA', as if it was something shocking and exotic, then rapidly digressing to how fat all North Americans are, how much we eat, about all the hamburgers and French fries and how lucky I am to be here now, saved from obesity, because Spaniards know how to eat. What pisses me off about this is not that they are in part right, but that they eat more than any North American I know and never seem to get fat. Spain is the only country where I have worried about falling into a food-induced coma, being force-fed by well-intentioned Spaniards. Yet, I cannot even squeeze an ass cheek into the stylish pants that all the Spanish women my age wear.

My first experience with serious Spanish eating was at a 40th birthday celebration of a friend of Fernando's. Guests were told to arrive at 11 am. Fernando was still not out of bed by 10 am and I was freaking out, bouncing around the apartment, threatening him with his life because he had to still shower, shave, get dressed and drive across the island. He kept telling me not to worry and not to rush, but I was near tears as we got in the car for the twenty-minute drive

116

at 10:55 am. "Lana, calm down. They told everyone to show up at 11 am so that everyone would be there by 12:30 pm. We are going to be the first ones there and we are not going to eat lunch until around 3 pm."

I should have believed my husband, being that he *is* Spanish, but could not override the fear and horror of arriving late, even for a social occasion.

When we finally got there, it was just the birthday boy, his wife and us. I was handed a beer with a smile, but, as the birthday boy turned, I saw him shoot his wife a look that said, 'why the hell are people showing up already and what are we going to do with them'.

Around 12:30 pm, people started showing up and plates started coming out, completely filling up the four-meter-long table. All the newcomers were handed a beer (Fernando and I were on our second beers because we had been there longer than everyone else). No one sat down; everyone just stood around the table socializing, drink in hand, picking away at the new arrivals. Fernando was pointing to different plates telling me what they were and what he thought I would like when I was given a glass of red wine.

As everyone finished their beer, it was substituted for a glass of red wine. As I was unconsciously trying to keep my meter of space around me, still not having adjusted to the fact that I do not own the space directly around me in Mediterranean countries as I do in the States (my German friend, who also owns the space around her, and I call Spaniards 'close talkers'), I accidentally tripped on one of various crates full of red wine. I whispered to Fernando, "In this huge house, he has nowhere to store his wine... He keeps it here in crates?"

Fernando gave me a look that I have seen parents give a very loved but very stupid child, squeezed my cheek and said, "*Cariño*, he has a wine cellar for his wine; this is the wine for the party."

I did a quick head count and then a quick bottle count, turned to Fernando and said, "Yeah right, there are more bottles of wine here than people."

He just continued to look at with me with love and amusement.

I was the only foreigner and everyone wanted to make sure that I tried everything the right way. If I was to eat cheese, pâté or Iberian ham, it had to be on a *pan con tomate*, toasted bread with a *diente* of garlic and tomato rubbed against it, dribbled with olive oil and sprinkled with salt. There was no point trying to explain that I did not want to fill up on bread, so I just paced myself, eating slowly and enjoying all the different flavors on top of my *pan con tomate*.

My wine glass was magically never empty and it is amazing how much more one can drink when you don't have the bottle in front of you to tell you exactly how much you have had to drink. I was getting tired after a few hours of so much eating, drinking and socializing and was looking forward to taking a hot shower in my severely buzzed state, lying down and waiting for digestion to start when I heard, "Help clear the table; lunch is almost ready."

I helped others clear the table as my ears rang because of the panic I was now experiencing. I thought it was coming to an end, but it had not even started yet. I was pacing myself with the food on the table thinking that that was all the food there would be. I could not believe that there was more, and that it was going to be more than what we had just ate. I remembered Fernando saying that we would eat lunch around 3 pm, but I had thought he was wrong when the table filled with massive amounts of food. I looked at my watch: 3:15 pm. Just when I thought it was over, it started again.

I tried to calm myself by thinking I could make it through another hour, two hours at most. I leaned over and whispered in Fernando's ear, "How much longer will the lunch go on?"

He whispered back, "We'll be lucky if we get out of here by 8 pm."

I searched his face for a joke because I could not honestly imagine that he was being serious, but saw no hint of jest.

The woman next to me must have sensed my distress because she kindly said, "Don't stress too much; the first plate is relatively light."

"First plate?" I turned to Fernando. "There is more than one?"

Those around me laughed, thinking that I was making a joke. Sheer terror was what they should have heard in my voice, but, being that Mediterranean people, I am convinced, have an extra gene that deals specifically with rapidly digesting and burning off food and alcohol, they thought my comment was a joke.

The woman next to me continued on about the *light* first plate. "Stuffed squid baked in the oven. This is a fundamental Menorcan recipe," she informed me.

I began to relax, thinking that maybe I could survive the first plate. Maybe the squid, which, indeed, is relatively light, was stuffed with vegetables. My hopes began to rise until the woman next to me began to tell me her family's recipe for stuffed squid. I only heard bits and pieces because, once she started, fear made my ears ring again. I caught, 'minced meat; half veal, half pork. *Sobrassada* (fermented sausage), garlic, parsley, bread crumbs, eggs, milk, olive oil and salt'. On what planet is that light?

The first plate was served and I stoically made my way through it. It was such a shame that I was already so full because it really was quite nice. I made a note to try it again if I ever decided that I wanted to resume eating in the future.

Fernando must have seen that I was on the verge of exploding, and said, "Lana, being that you are the only foreigner at the table, everyone is watching you to see if you like these Menorcan dishes. If you don't eat everything on your plate, it would be kind of an insult to them, so please try. I promise that we will never eat again."

I wondered what he was preparing me for as the cutlery was set for the second plate. I swear I almost fainted when I saw what the second dish was. It was absolutely impossible that we were going to eat that after what we had already eaten. I looked at the utensils and the knife was sufficiently sharp to cut my jugular vein. A nice quick slash and my suffering would be over.

Somehow, I mustered the courage to live and confront the second dish in the center of the table, which was about to be cut up and served.

Two entire (meaning just that) suckling piglets were in a very large dish surrounded by garlic and potatoes... little baby snout, little baby curly tail and all.

"I want the ear... I want the ear," a little Menorcan boy of about six years of age yelled.

His father, who was helping to cut up the wee little baby pigs, smiled proudly, cut the ear of the suckling, placed it in front of his son, slapped the boy on the back and said, 'just like his dad', with a ridiculously large grin on his face. I have no idea why eating a baby pig's ear was something to be proud of, but decided to let it go.

"Lana, do you want an ear?"

"No, no," I almost screamed.

"How about a snout? It's the best part, so tender and gelatinous."

Vomiting my response would have been the most descriptive answer, but I settled for a severe shake of the head while grinding my teeth trying to keep the bile back. I am not a finicky eater and am always game to try new things; however, I was currently more full than I had ever been in my entire life... painfully so. I seriously was asking myself if it was possible to pass out from over eating when I was offered the 'gelatinous snout'. Oh, why had the Roman tradition of the *vomitorium* been discontinued? I am sure it has to do with my suspicions of Mediterranean people having an extra gene. *Survival of the fittest.* There must have, at one point, been a mutation in some of the Mediterranean people's genes allowing some to eat vast amounts of food and drink vast amounts of alcohol. These quantities of food and alcohol killed off the ones who did not have this mutation. Therefore, the Roman *vomitoriums* fell into disuse, and today, Mediterranean people can eat and drink to no end without getting drunk or becoming overweight.

I made a vow that if I was to survive the day without death by exploding, I would write to all travel guides in the USA begging them to put a warning about this phenomenon so that other naïve foreigners like myself could plan out some sort of strategy if invited to a Mediterranean meal.

I was given a large chunk of some part of the suckling. My eyes glazed over and I went into automatic mode in order to complete the task at hand. Cut, fork, mouth, chew and swallow. Cut, fork, mouth, chew, and swallow. I looked at my plate with a deep pride. I had done it! The impossible. I turned to Fernando and told him about my success. When I turned back, there was another equally large chuck of sucking on my plate.

After conquering the second chunk of meat (this time, I ate extremely slowly so that there was no possibility of having a third helping of the second dish), the birthday boy brought out a cake. I cannot honestly say what was in it. I was now entering my food- and alcohol-induced coma. After forcing the cake down, coffee was finally served. I stared in amazement at other guests who took a second helping of birthday cake to have with their coffee. It was now 6:20 pm and I was glad for once that Fernando had made an error in his Spanish time estimation. He had said we would probably leave around 8 pm. It was almost 6:30 pm and we were finishing up our coffee.

Fernando must have mistaken my excitement at our nearing departure for nervousness or anxiousness because he said, "Yeah, this part I like the least, as well."

I was going to ask what he was talking about when I saw the wife of the birthday boy bring forth a huge tray loaded with bottles of alcohol, followed by her son, who carried all of the necessary sodas for mixing along with a bucket of ice. While I was staring in disbelief at the bottles, which implied that there was still more drinking to do, instruments were somehow magically produced.

Fernando grumbled, "At least two hours of putting up with drunken singing and then we can make an attempt to leave."

Every time I thought it was over, it started again. I finally resigned myself to the fact that it was never going to end.

A gin and tonic was put in my hands and the singing began. The majority of the songs played were typical Menorcan songs and the instruments being used were a guitar and a keyboard for lack of piano. It was all very authentic, but I was past the point of desiring to be part of and see true Menorcan culture. All I wanted to do was to be carried to my house, put in the shower, dried off and put to bed.

Fernando does not sing, dance or play a musical instrument, so he joined me in drinking and observing. Potato chips and nuts were produced to munch on while drinking our hard alcoholic beverage so that no one would go hungry. At 9 pm, Fernando and I bid our farewells and were the first ones to leave the party.

I ate only fruit for the entire week that followed.

We were later told that the singing and drinking went on until 11 pm, when hefty baguettes were produced and promptly eaten so that no one would drive home drunk. Yes, it was reassuring to know that, after twelve hours of drinking, no one drove home drunk because they ate a sandwich beforehand.

9

Houseguests

"Hola."

"Hi… Lana? It's me, Christy. Your mom gave me your number."

"It's good to hear from you; how are you?" I asked, using my polite, formal tone that I use for strangers, when someone is angry or for acquaintances (basically for people who are not friends).

Christy and boyfriend were acquaintances. I knew them both in high school and we had chatted a few times when I had gone back home for a visit.

"I am great, thanks. So we finally did it. We made time to come visit you in Menorca."

I really enjoyed how that was phrased as if it was a favor to me, something that I had been begging and hoping for. Honestly, I do not ever remember extending an invitation. I quickly scanned my brain and came up with us having a quick chat in the supermarket where we ran into each other on my last visit home. I remember her asking about Menorca and me replying something like, "Yeah, it is a beautiful island, but I don't get to see much of it because I work so much during the summer."

To this, I remember her saying something like, "Well, who would have ever thought that you would end up in a tropical paradise?"

"Mediterranean paradise," I had corrected.

"Well, Chad and I will just have to come out one of these days and see how it is."

To this, I had made a noise, a polite tonal intonation that I make when I am just trying to make the conversation easy, but really don't have anything to say on the matter.

We said our goodbyes and that was that. I had never thought about it again. Because I was so caught off guard, I really did not know how to deal with the situation. And I am horrible at saying no.

I heard myself ask, "Really, for how long and when?"

At this point, I heard Fernando jump up off the sofa in the living room and run towards the door. He threw it open and started waving his hands, urgently mouthing one word over and over: 'NO'.

"For three weeks in August. With the plane ticket being so expensive and all, coming for less than three weeks would be just silly."

"Silly indeed," my mouth said. "Three weeks in August," I echoed back, trying to understand.

At this point, Fernando dropped to his knees, pushed his hands together in a steeple form, begging me to take action. I marveled at his ability to understand English when it suited him. It reminded me of my dog, Bruce, who was selectively deaf.

"We know you have a lot of work in August; your mom told us that it was your busiest month, but that is the only time Chad could get time off. Anyways, you won't even know we're there."

So that confirmed it. They were planning on staying in my house. Up until that moment, I realized I had been hoping that they were going to ask if I had any suggestions on places to stay.

Fernando must have seen it on my face because his hands in the steeple, begging position changed to a pistol shape, which he put under his chin and was now committing suicide over and over again.

*   *   *   *

Living in a Mediterranean paradise can make a person very popular. It has caused many family members and friends to realize how much they *truly* miss me. I have realized (too late) that sending postcards while traveling is fine, but sending postcards from where you live is both dangerous and unwise. Sending postcards while traveling is both fun and nice. It lets your friends and family feel that, even though you are off having fun, you are still thinking of them. Sending postcards from where you live is also fine as long as you live in a place where no one would want to visit you. It makes others think, 'how nice of them to think of me and how fortunate I am not to be there'. However, sending postcards from an island surrounded by crystal-clear, warm saltwater that gently laps at hundreds of virgin beaches will be selectively interpreted as an invitation whether it was meant as one or not.

*   *   *   *

Unpleasant things that houseguests have done apart from causing me stress:

Broke the clutch on my 'newish' car, clogged my toilet, shorted out my electricity, streaked my white walls with blue and red body paint, daily used up all the hot water in the shower right before I came home after a twelve-hour day, drank all of my wine, ate all of my expensive cheese that I no longer had time to go out and buy at the farm on the other side of the island, left me to baby sit and feed three children after working twelve hours, told me that I am not respectable because I do not speak Catalan (while drinking my wine!), repeatedly used the only internet connection in the house at night, which is the only time that I am able to use it and need to use it for work, disrespected and pissed off staff workers, loudly played horrible music, caused our electricity bill to triple, and complained to me about their profound disappointment when finding out there was no *flamenco* dancing on Menorca.

* * * *

The best type of houseguest is the self-entertaining houseguest who will not bother you all day long, but is at home (and already showered so that there will be enough hot water in the tank for you when you come home from work) when you get home after a long day with a few suggestions about dinner plans so that you do not have to think after a hard day at work and can choose from the options presented to you that they will then prepare. This type of houseguest will usually go out daily and buy fresh fruits and vegetables, fresh bread, local cheese and a different type of wine each day to experiment with. This type of houseguest will most likely have a positive or amusing story of their day's adventure waiting for you once you are set with a glass of wine and a nibble of cheese with your feet propped up.

Unfortunately, this is about ten percent of houseguests. The other vast majority of houseguests are the kind who will call you at work throughout the day asking 'when you will be home? What is there to do?' They will tell you that they are bored, that it is very unproductive that everything is closed between 2-6 pm, and that there is no fast food in your town. This type of houseguest will be waiting for the click of the door handle and will pounce on you the second you walk through the door asking if 'you want to go out and have a drink' or 'go out and do something' after your twelve-hour day. This type of houseguest will eat all your food, drink all your wine and never do the dishes. This type of houseguest will tell you all the reasons why where they are from is better than where you live.

My friend, Carisa, and her boyfriend, Scott, fall into type one: the self-entertaining houseguests, even though they contributed three items on the unpleasant-things list above.

When Carisa and Scott decided to come to Menorca, Scott bought Carisa a Mediterranean cookbook. The fact alone that Carisa graduated from one of the best culinary schools in the USA is enough to make her a wonderful houseguest. She had a few pages marked as dinners she wanted to prepare for us all. Unfortunately, Fernando does not like many Mediterranean basics such as cheese, olives, onion and garlic. Carisa wanted to dazzle my husband with her culinary abilities and surprise him with her flexibility that allowed her to master food from his own culture. But the little detail that Fernando does not like many of the staples of the Mediterranean diet made things a bit complicated.

Carisa and I went through the book again and selected new dinners. The one that we decided on for the coming night was Catalan pizza… cheeseless! We made a list and she was going to go shopping the next day while we were at work. Around noon, I received a phone call. "Lana, how do you say yeast?"

The evil word again. I do not cook often and yeast is definitely something that I had never cooked with in Spain, or anywhere else, for that matter, so I did not have the Spanish word on the tip of my tongue and, after my other unfortunate experience with the word yeast, I was not willing to make a venture. My dear friend said that she would figure something out and not to worry.

I was greeted in my doorway by wonderful smells. I walked into the kitchen and Carisa had a long green pepper over a flame while Scott grated cheese. I looked at Carisa questionably and she gave me a quick shake of the head. "Honey, how much cheese does it call for?"

"That should be enough; thanks for helping... You know I hate grating cheese." Scott, now feeling like a good boyfriend, walked out of the kitchen smiling, leaving us girls to carry on.

While I looked at the pile of grated cheese, Carisa said, "He had half the cheese grated before I even noticed what he was doing. He was trying to be so helpful that I didn't have the heart to tell him that the recipe calls for no cheese. Plus, I don't want to discourage his helping behavior, which is rare enough as it is."

We laughed and began munching on the grated cheese.

"Why is it that the same cheese grated tastes so much better than un-grated?"

Carisa pondered this for a moment and said, "I think it must be one of those universal mystery things that science has yet to figure out."

"Yeah, along with, why is it that every time men try to be helpful, they always screw something up?"

"Yes, see Exhibit #1: grated cheese."

Pouring myself a glass of red wine from the bottle that Carisa had uncorked before my arrival for this reason, I told Carisa, "Fernando just thinks he doesn't like cheese. He always eats cheese on pizza and loves cheese sauces as long as I tell him that they are cream sauces. The same goes for onions and garlic. He loves them in everything as long as I mince them small enough so that he cannot identify what they are. Olives are the only thing that he *really* does not like."

"It's the same with Scott and onions," Carisa confided in me as we lightly sprinkled what was left of the grated cheese on the handmade pizza dough, so that Scott would not find out that his efforts were for nothing.

"So, did you ever figure out how to say yeast?"

She grabbed the box that said '*levadura*'. "I used my extensive Spanish skills... I said, '*pan*' while I worked the imaginary dough in the air in front of the lady at the supermarket, followed by my hands rising and if they were the dough. She looked at me like I was crazy, but gave me this box and it looks about right."

"Ah, that was the evil word... I must have repressed it," I said, and then told her about my mushrooms in my private parts experience.

This caused an explosive laugh from my friend who had, unfortunately, just taken a sip of wine. She assured me that wine coming out the nose burned.

The Catalan pizza was a big success, cheese and all.

The next day, I asked them if they wanted to catch a ride with me to work, go to the beach nearby, and use my car to drive around. They eagerly accepted. I had to stop by the small supermarket in the town of Es Mercadal on the way to work and Carisa and Scott accompanied me in. I bought a few items that I needed and wandered back to the butcher to get some *jamón serrano* for them to try later on. The butcher had a strange look on his face and I glanced to the right and saw why... Carisa and Scott were taking pictures of the skinned rabbits and chickens with their heads still attached. I looked at the butcher with a helpless expression and said, "Friends of mine visiting from the USA."

The butcher replied, "I should have known."

Carisa looked at me and I said I would explain later. I ordered my 300 grams of Spanish ham and was out of there. In the car, I told her that the butcher must have a strange opinion of people from the USA. "We don't get many tourists here from the USA, so his opinion of us North Americans is based solely on you two taking pictures of his meat and of me asking for dick every time I go in."

Carisa's head snapped around and her eyes bulged as she asked me in a scandalized tone that she is so good at, "What!"

"It is not as good of a story as you might think. Fernando does not eat much red meat, so I always get chicken when I go to the butcher. The word for chicken is *pollo*. The word for dick in Spain is *polla*. Being that my husband is Spanish, and men love to talk about their *pollas*, I hear the word *polla* more often than chicken. Every time I go to the butcher, I repeat to myself like a mantra beforehand, '*pollo, pollo, pollo, pollo*', but, of course, *polla* always comes out." I often feel like I have Tourette's Syndrome when speaking Spanish. I know the word that I need to say, I struggle with it in my head and the wrong one pops out of my mouth every time. "And," I continued, "it is not the technical term that I ask for… It is the equally vulgar term for penis as dick is. So yes, I ask for dick and you take pictures of dead rabbits and chickens. I could see where people may think that we are a bit strange."

"We are strange? They had un-refrigerated milk in the supermarket. How can you have un-refrigerated milk?" asked Scott. "It was on the shelf next to cans!"

I explained that I was not sure, but that it must have something to do with how it is pasteurized. The un-refrigerated milk is much creamier. The first time I tried it, I thought that I had mistakenly grabbed a bottle of cream. But I do admit, I am a bit suspicious of how milk can have such a long, un-refrigerated shelf life.

The next stop was to get fresh bread. I called ahead to order the bread needed for the museum the night before. They always have my bread ready in a bag waiting for me, so all I have to do is run in and grab it. My first year here, I would search ten minutes for correct parking, walk five minutes to get to the bread store and then walk five minutes back to my car. After months of observation, I realized that putting on your hazard lights while illegally parked, or while stopping in the middle of the road, seems to be perfectly acceptable as long as it is for not too long. I have even seen local police walk right past cars very illegally parked with their blinking hazard lights on. It seemed that, instead of calling more attention to the illegally parked car, it gave it a sort of invisibility cloak.

I decided one day I would give this a try. I stopped in the center of the street, put on my hazard lights, jumped out of my car, dashed into the bread store, grabbed my bag, dashed back to my car and took off. I was expecting honking horns, people flipping me off, etc. However, this has never happened. I give appreciative waves when I am dashing back to my car for their patience and understanding as to why I am cutting off traffic. I have only ever received polite, understanding waves back. In my defense, I only do this on small side roads.

I proceeded with my normal routine. As I jumped back in the car and pushed the button, deactivating my invisibility cloak, I looked over to see Carisa's disapproving look. "You just stopped traffic to get your bread and there was even a policeman watching. I was so embarrassed when he made eye contact with me. Will he send you a ticket in the mail?"

I laughed and shook my head. It used to drive me completely crazy when I saw people do this or when I was waiting behind them. But now that I have started doing it, it does not bother me at all. I am conforming. When in Rome…

We went through the rest of Es Mercadal and started on the twisty road to the Cape of Cavalleria. I started my typical 'drive to the Cape of Cavalleria speech', pointing out the swooping round hay bales, the whitewashed farmhouses with the small windows with green shutters. "The whitewash on all of the older houses is ground-up lime mixed with water. It is a pain because you have to do it every year, but it is really cheap. When you mix it, it starts to boil. Once it is done boiling, it is ready to use. I paint parts of Santa Teresa, the farm house where the museum is, every year. I hate painting with lime because it dries your skin out while you use it. But it has been a part of life for so long in Menorca, and many parts of Spain, that it makes me feel like a special guest allowed to take part in the history here… chapped hands and all. I am sure that people for hundreds of years have been bitching about painting with lime. The windows are small because they are more practical, especially with the winds we have on the island that plaster glass surfaces with salt and sneak their way in through the cracks. The *tramontana* wind can find its way into any northern surface. All of the windows that face the north in Santa Teresa are very small and the northern wall is about a meter thick. The shutters on all of the windows are green because that is the color of shutter that Menorca as an island uses. Something to do with the British occupation of the island. Mallorca has brown shutters and Ibiza blue. Almost everyone goes along with….."

My monolog was interrupted by eleven baby pigs running down the road. They were trotting down the center and not veering to the side. I followed their little curly tails slowly for about a kilometer, but could not get them to veer off the road. Every time there was a space in the rock wall, we would jump out and try to herd them there, but to no avail. The little baby pigs continued to tiredly trot down the road. "Shit, I hope there is no oncoming traffic this early in the morning. If someone comes around the corner quickly, they are going to hit them."

"Well, we won't let their death be in vain; we can always eat them," Scott added helpfully.

Luckily, we were on a straight stretch when an oncoming car approached. As we neared, I was relieved to see that it was the farmer of Cavalleria's wife. We cross paths every morning and it took me three years of waving frantically each morning to finally get a wave back. This baby pig experience happened after the returning of the waves and she slowed down and greeted me with a smile. The baby pigs, not knowing where to go now that there were large metal things on both sides, went a bit crazy and scattered in all directions. Fortunately, the majority were now off the road. I told her they had been trotting in front of me for over a kilometer and she started calling the nearby farms in an attempt to locate the owners of the piglets. Now that they were off the road, and someone else was in control of the situation (though I never was, just forcing the wee-babies to trot in front of me not knowing what else to do), we continued on to work, now about twenty minutes late. Luckily, Fernando understands and accepts being late due to livestock in the road or by being stuck behind a tractor. There is not much you can do in these kinds of situations except wait and go slow.

We finally reached the cape and I parked in the parking of the Ecomuseum. My guest gave the appropriate 'ooohhhhss' and 'aaaaahhhhhss' when taking in the panoramic. I pointed out the natural port, the local fishermen's boats, the lighthouse, the British defense tower and the archaeological sites where Fernando was working. I opened the side door of the museum and handed them a map of the area that they could busy themselves with while I opened everything up. "Coffee will be ready in about half an hour."

This seemed to please them and off they went. How nice to have good houseguests who know they would only be in my way while I opened.

They hiked around the cape for a while and came back when I was finishing up. We had coffee together and they let me know that they were going to use my car only for today to find a rental car so that I could have my car in case of an emergency. What lovely, considerate houseguests; I continued to think this until I received a call from a friend. "Lana, did you know your car is alongside main road, unoccupied?"

The blood drained from my body, but I was still thinking this may be a joke.

"Are you sure it is my car, Yago?"

"Yeap, no other red Nissan Almera on the island is that covered in dirt."

"*Mierda!* My friends had it and I have no idea what happened."

"Ha ha, Fernando is going to love this. Call me if you need a ride."

Why is it that fear makes you feel like you are floating? Pins pricked my cheeks, the soles of my feet and my fingertips. Fear is white pin pricks and floating. First, I was worried that my friends had wrecked my car and my fear was of Fernando's reaction. Fernando is not a violent person. However, his calm, silent anger is equally, if not more, terrifying than violence. The white pin pricks increased their intensity when I started to consider what had become of Carisa and Scott. Menorca is not a dangerous place, but where were they?

After an eternity of twenty-five minutes of floating, Carisa peeked a sheepish head through the museum door.

"Lana, um... um... the clutch on your car... um... is not working."

I let out a huge sigh of relief, and said, "I am glad that is all it is. A friend told me he saw my car along the road and I was really beginning to get concerned."

"Lana, you're upset about your car; you are just trying to hide it so I won't feel bad."

I reassured her that I was not upset with her and that I felt bad that my car chose to break when she was driving it. I recommended that we all have a gin and tonic... not so much for their sake, but more for mine because Fernando was due to show up in about a half an hour and I would have to explain what had happened. As we sipped our gin and tonics, Carisa explained that luckily it had happened after they had picked up the rental car and Scott was following her.

"After about a half an hour of not knowing what to do with your car, the police showed up. They kept motioning for us to put something on... like a jacket. We had no idea what they wanted, especially because we had no jackets, until one of them took my keys from me, opened the trunk and took out a reflective vest."

I choked on my gin and tonic, laughing. When I first moved to Spain, I thought that there were some ridiculously cautious and paranoid people. People who stopped alongside the road for whatever reason, to change a tire, to help another stranded vehicle, etc., all put on reflective vests when outside their car. Even joggers who jogged in the evenings wore reflective vests. Finally, someone told me that everyone does this because it is the law.

Carisa checked her watch about ten times within a two-minute period of time and I knew she was thinking the same thing that I was; Fernando was due to show up at any minute. I did not see the point of all of us suffering, so I told them to go home and that Fernando could take me home, call a tow truck and do whatever else was needed after I closed up. Carisa and Scott gave me grateful looks and speed-walked to the parking lot.

Fernando dealt with the crisis better than I thought he would. He quietly smoldered, but that was about it. He called a tow truck. Fortunately, the nearest town was where our mechanic is located, so it was not a big deal. Carisa and Scott sincerely offered to pay, but Fernando kindly declined. I was very impressed with Fernando until he started telling everyone that Yankees don't know how to drive stick-shifts. This then progressed to Fernando telling everyone that there are only automatic clutches in the USA and that is why Yankees don't know how to drive stick-shifts. The amazing thing is that everyone believed him despite the fact that I am from the USA and said repeatedly that it isn't so and that I have only ever driven a stick-shift.

*   *   *   *

The summer after my friends visited, Fernando's recently divorced and depressed friend and his three children came to stay the entire month of August. Now, when the topic of houseguests arises, Fernando says absolutely nothing. A broken car was a mere little inconvenience in comparison to that August of pure hell.

Fernando and I no longer have a phone line in our house. Anyone who needs to call us can do so on our cell phones. I make my international phone calls via my computer. If anyone asks why we chose to do this, we lie and say, "Because we rented out our flat and are living on our small, one-bed sailboat."

10

Becoming Spanish

When I moved to Spain, I was more concerned with mastering the language, taking in the culture and learning to live a whole new way of life than I was with the actual bureaucracy of living in a new country. I should have known better after the mountains of paperwork and numerous trips to the Spanish consulate in San Francisco just to obtain a study abroad visa for a semester stay in Spain the previous year. However, I decided to push those memories far to the hidden depths of my brain that contain all of the stuff that I should have at the very front (like not canceling registration on my car that I left at my mom's house, unpaid parking tickets, etc.) and decided to convince myself that just having my Californian marriage certificate, my proof that I was married to a Spaniard, was enough to stay in the country.

Every once in a while, the fact that I knew better would creep to the peripheral of my cranium and cause sleepless nights, until it actually made its way to the front and decided to stay and nag. Unfortunately, this was a year after I had been living in Spain.

On our next trip to Barcelona, I went to the US Embassy and told a very helpful and kind lady my position. The expression on her face was not encouraging and, when she said 'you are kind of screwed', I knew for sure that I was in for trouble. She explained to me that someone from the USA can visit Spain for up to three months without a visa, but, after that, a visa is required. What I should have done was gotten a visa before coming to Spain with my husband and initiated my residency paperwork right away. What I needed to do now was go back to the USA and get a visa from the Spanish consulate. However, now that I had violated my allotted time in Spain, it was very possible that I would not be allowed back into Europe for two years.

I was devastated and frustrated by my own ignorance. I had thought I could just wonder through life like a gypsy and that luck would just come my way and take care of me (which it pretty much always has). I began to think of all the ways I could beat the system. I thought about *losing* my passport and getting a new one with hopefully a new number that would not reflect my extended stay in Spain. The more I thought about this, the more I warmed to the idea.

Once we were back in Menorca, I started talking to other immigrants who I suspected to be in Spain in not the most official manner. Supporting my theory, many told me that *losing* your passport was the way to go because, on entering most European countries, they just look over the stamps, not like in the USA where they control everything by electronically scanning your passport, documenting the milliseconds of foreigner's stay within the country.

Maria (we will call her this while speaking of her illegal activities), my friend, an Argentinean, told me that she had *lost* her passport five times and, therefore, was able to visit her family in Argentina and get back into Spain year after year without having to worry about a visa that most likely would not be granted to her anyway. "I don't feel bad about it. How many Spaniards came running to us in the 30s, 40s and 50s? We welcomed them all with open arms. And, we shipped meat to Spain to help starving Spanish citizens during the 'years of hunger' after the civil war. But when our country has an economic crisis, Spain turns it's back on us and makes it almost impossible for us to stay and work so that we can help feed our families."

Her reasoning seemed well justified and I felt myself redden because I had no such justifications for being an illegal immigrant. She must have seen my embarrassment because she added in attempts to console me, "But don't worry, there are two types of immigrants in Spain, or that is at least how a great many Spaniards view it. There are the immigrants from Central and South America, the Middle East, Africa and Eastern European. These are the undesirable immigrants. Then there are the rest, which are the acceptable immigrants. And the most acceptable are, even if they talk shit about them, Northerners... American and European. I bet they did not even stamp your passport when you came into the country."

This did not have the consoling effect that my dear friend, Maria, had intended; quite the opposite, in fact. I felt like a horrible racist for just being viewed in this way and even more so for the fleeting hope that was sneaking over me. Maybe I would not be banned for two years. Maybe my blonde hair, white skin and nationality would get me out of this situation. I hated myself for thinking this and tried to convince myself that I wanted the strictest punishment for my illegal immigrant status so I could also bitch about how unfair the world was to me. But, as much as I tried, I could not convince myself that this is what I really wanted. Yes, I wanted the world to be fair... but only in my favor. Yes, I know I am going to Hell.

Maria was now curious as to the unfairness of the world and wanted to see if, indeed, they had or had not stamped my passport on entering the country. In my apartment, I took my passport out of my nightstand table and started to flip through it while Maria looked over my shoulder. We flipped through the different pages and the different stamps. There was no stamp from the airport in Spain that I had landed in a year ago. We both cheered, and I felt instantly guilty that Maria was so sincerely happy that I had not been stamped when knowing perfectly well that she would get stamped each and every time coming into Spain, causing her to have to pay for another passport. We were two Americans cheering about the same thing. One from the south and one from the north. One with a passport stamped on entry to Spain and one not.

My cheering died quickly and Maria noticed the change in my face while I contemplated this, and said, "Don't feel too bad. The reason they control me more than you is because they think that you are coming to be a tourist and will go back home shortly while they think that I am coming to stay and work illegally."

I tried and failed at a smile.

"Hey, don't worry. They were right about me, just wrong about you."

This time, I managed the smile that Maria and her good humor deserved.

After consulting with a few more immigrants who laughed at my fears of being deported from Menorca, I decided to go and ask what I would need in order to attain my residency. I was told that the Balearic Islands were easier than other places to attain residency because the islands had not yet been inundated with the numbers of immigrants that the rest of Spain had. Even though I had been guaranteed that I would not be deported, even if discovered, I was not thrilled to find out that the place I had to go to ask about and apply for residency was the main police headquarters.

As I walked towards the police station, I chanted my mantra, 'I have no stamp; they have no proof; I have no

stamp; they have no proof', over and over. I pushed open
the doors. Seated was a man who I guessed to be from Peru
or Ecuador, who looked completely devastated or stoned; I
was not sure which. I hoped for stoned instead of
devastated while waiting for deportation. I thought to
myself, *oh shit,* but forced myself to proceed to the counter
anyway and asked where I could find information on
attaining residency. The policeman looked me up and
down, smiled and told me that I had to go outside, around
the corner and through the other door. "This side of the
building is for the bad guys and you don't look like a bad
guy to me."

I thanked him and quickly exited, trying not to laugh at
his error in judgment. With there hardly being any crime on
the island, my illegal status could almost qualify me as a
bad guy.

I walked around to the other side and was told to go to
the first floor and wait in the line that was trickling down
the stairs. People of all different nationalities came out of
the office on the first floor, passing me on the stairs, some
smiling and some holding back tears. When my turn came,
I walked into the office and my hopes immediately fell
when I saw the lady attending to us immigrants hoping for
residency. She had the most bitch-face and sick-of-the-
world aura about her that I had ever seen. I was not longer
worried about being deported; I was more concerned about
laser beams shooting out of her eyes. I sat in front of her
and felt like an insecure little girl who does not know
whether or not to speak until spoken to.

A '*si?*' from her gave me the permission that she was
waiting for me to speak. I explained that I had just arrived
in Menorca with my Spanish husband, that we had been
married in California and that I was wondering what I
needed to do in order to gain my residency so that we could
live here together and so that I could get a job working

legally. She pulled out a paper and told me that I needed to fill out the box with my name now and the rest of the front side later. I wrote my name in the correct boxes and handed it back to her. "Your other last name?" she asked.

I told her that I only had one. She gave me a skeptical look and said, "This is my first time with an American… You guys only have one last name?"

I explained that as a rule, yes, and it is the father's last name, which his wife also takes on in place of her own once she is married. She mumbled under her breath that sounded something like she had thought Spaniards were male chauvinists. I had to agree; I like the Spanish system better; no one changes their names and children get the last name of both the father and the mother. The only thing that I do not agree on is that it is usually the father's last name first, followed by the mother's. It should obviously go the other way around… It is a much better bet on the certainty of your mother than your father.

While I was running this over in my head, she had flipped the page over and started checking a column of small boxes on the left that ran from top to bottom. After each box, there were phrases that I could not clearly see. After checking only half of the boxes, she handed the page back to me and told me that I needed to bring her all of the items that she had marked, with a photocopy of each.

So the crucial moment had arrived. "Do I have to go back to my country to get a visa?"

"You are recently married… Do you want to be separated from your husband for the time that would take?"

"No, not really."

"Well, as long as you are within your three-month tourist visa and do not leave the country until all of this paperwork is completed, I see no need for you to do so."

I sucked in a preparatory breath, hoped that I had no visible nervous hives and said, "I have one slight problem.

Although I just arrived in Spain, I realized before coming here that my passport was not stamped on entry. I have no way of proving how long I have been here."

She looked at me and let one of those very uncomfortable and knowing silences fall between us. I was expecting to now be vaporized by her laser beams. Finally, she let out a long sigh (just before tumbleweeds started rolling across the floor between us) and said, "Just get the paperwork I marked done as quickly as possible; do not leave the country or compromise yourself in anyway."

I thanked her and thanked her, and left almost running out the door before she could change her mind.

While driving home, I considered my first impression of this woman who now held my fate in her hands. Having a bitch-face is an unfortunate thing. I have known people with bitch-faces and some are bitches, while others are completely wonderful people. I believe that I have a very open face and that is why people often think that I am nicer and more social than I am. This can also be unfortunate. Having a face that does not match you can be problematic. On reflection, I realized that this residency woman was not as bad as I had first thought. She was actually, to a degree, nice. Maybe the unsmiling face and the sick-of-the-world aura was a helpful tool for those seeking her assistance. She gave no false hope to anyone. Everyone thought they were screwed when they walked in. And, of course, some are. I wondered if having a bitch-face was a requirement of her job position. I can see the benefits.

I took a wrong turn when leaving the police station, but was so happy that I could still apply for residency and without having to go back to my country for more paperwork, that, instead of cursing or getting angry, my normal reaction, I thought that surely taking the wrong turn must have happened for a reason... maybe I had avoided an accident or red lights, etc. I wish that I could always be so ridiculously positive.

When I got home, I looked over the checked boxes on the paper that I had been handed in the office and noticed that the ones she did not check were the ones dealing with interviews and visitations to our home. While I was happy that I did not have to go through those ordeals, guilt started to gnaw at my cheerful mood. What was it about me that made Bitch-face think that I would not marry for papers? Did I look in love? Do I not look like a devious or desperate person? Or was it something else? Maria's words came back to me. I tried to block them out by considering the likely possibility that Fernando and I would have failed the interview anyway. Friends had told me that they can come up with unexpected questions:

What color is your spouses' toothbrush? Failed: Fernando does not even know what color his own toothbrush is, let alone mine. This is why his is on one side of the counter and mine on the other, though he is not aware of the reason. I devised this system after repeatedly finding my toothbrush already wet in the morning.

What side of the bed do you sleep on? Failed: Fernando, though extremely intelligent, always mixes up left and right. It should be fifty-fifty, but he always seems to say or understand the wrong one. I now point when giving directions.

What is your spouses' favorite food? Failed: neither of us have favorite foods (not a very believable answer).

What is your spouses' birthday? Failed: Fernando does not remember dates very well (unless they are a thousand years or more old). I start giving him subtle warnings a week before my birthday or our anniversary so that he does not forget. I also have to announce to him his own birthday and age. One day in June, I went to work and all of the staff smiled at me and said, "Happy birthday!"

Some even had gifts. I told them that it was not my birthday… my birthday was in March, three months earlier. They all looked annoyed. Fernando had told them all at the beginning of the week that my birthday was June 9th. I waited for him to tell me happy birthday, but he did not. He had forgotten that he had told the staff that it was my birthday. I asked, "Aren't you going to wish me happy birthday?"

He looked panicked and said, "I am sooooo sorry. Happy birthday!"

I patted his shoulder and said it was okay because I loved the day long boat excursion and romantic dinner that he had given me three months earlier on my other birthday. My *real* birthday is March 6th. My *work* birthday is now June 9th.

What is your spouses' favorite singer? Failed: Fernando has no idea that what I listen to most is Joni Mitchell, Dar Williams, Ani Defranco and the likes. He calls all my music lesbian music. And I can imagine him saying something like this in the interview, not realizing that any suggestions of me being a lesbian would not be good for me getting my residency via marriage to him.

I started to feel a little better after realizing that the interview would have been a death blow to my residency attempts. If a married couple cannot even pass the marriage interview, I cannot even fathom how two strangers could do it. Or maybe it is a trick. Any couple that is actually able to pass the marriage interview is suspect.

The boxes that were checked were very reasonable and doable. I had to have a complete photocopy of my passport and produce the original for comparison when turning it in. A photocopy of my husband's ID card and the original. Two passport-sized photos. A document from the city hall stating that I was, indeed, living in my town, Es Migjorn Gran, and filed it as my place of residence (which all I had to do was go to the town hall and tell them that I lived there, giving them my address). My birth certificate and marriage certificate signed by the Secretary of State, attaining the Apostille that makes it valid here in Europe and both officially translated to Spanish. After a bit of looking around on the internet (to find out what an Apostille was and how to get one), I was able to send my papers to where they needed to go. It was now just a matter of waiting for them to come back to me and have them officially translated.

Everything was going according to plan until my dear husband surprised me with two tickets to Argentina. 'Don't leave the country', Bitch-face had said. Fernando's enthusiasm did not falter when I explained this. He was convinced that I would have no problem getting back into the county. More importantly, the tickets were non-refundable.

The month-long trip to Argentina was amazing. We completely relaxed drinking unbelievably good and cheap Argentinean wine and eating ridiculous amounts of red meat. I now understand why there are no Argentinean wines on the shelves of supermarkets in the USA. They would take over the market with their wine-producing area, Mendoza, enjoying almost the same latitude as Napa Valley, just on the bottom half of the world. Same climate (just opposite times), but a whole lot cheaper. Oh… and the beef cooked in BBQ fashion, which they call *asado*. The difference in flavor of grain-fed-and-locked-in-stalls cows to pasture-fed cows is striking. Happy cows taste better.

If I am a cow in my next life, I would first choose to be a cow in India where I would be considered sacred. If I did not behave well enough in this life to merit India cow status, I would settle for being an Argentinean cow where I could roam enormous pastures, drink sweet, fresh water, and enjoy breathtaking views before I met my end. I would meet my end not tragically, knowing that my death would not be in vain, that my pasture-fed body would become a wonderful *asado*.

Weighing a few kilos more, we headed back to Spain. On the twelve-hour flight home, I began to get nervous. Fernando had pointed out that I still had no stamp on my passport, so there should be no problem. However, I began to conjure up every way they could possibly bust me. Maybe they would look at the date of departure from the USA and start to wonder. Maybe they secretly controlled passports via chips, but did not let you know they were doing it. Maybe they had, indeed, stamped my passport, but with a certain type of ink that only showed up under special lights. Fernando was very amused by my paranoiac imagination and decided that only someone from the USA, or someone who had watched way too many action movies, could come up with so many improbable scenarios dealing with passport control.

My anxiety mounted as we disembarked and I was almost in tears by the time Fernando and I had to separate, him going to the quick European Union line for passport control, while I went to one of the five very slow lines that attended people from the rest of the world. Around me were mostly the people who had flown from Argentina to Spain on the same flight, the non-Europeans.

I started to pay attention to the people in front of me when I was about five people back from my turn. It was the turn of a girl around my age. She had started crying. The man controlling passports did not give her passport back and pointed to a corner, where she went and continued to sob. The same thing happened to the next two girls in my line. I started to panic. I saw that no other passport control officer was causing problems and many were smiling and laughing with the people they were dealing with. I thought about switching lines, but was worried that would call even more attention to myself. It was now my turn and I walked up to the booth with my ears ringing in fear. The blue cover of my passport must have had a consolatory effect, changing his mood, because he did not even look over my stamps, just flipped to a blank page and stamped me. Well, at least he stamped me. At least I could tell Maria that. Maybe I would leave out the part that he had scrutinized over the Argentinean passports before me and had even detain three girls before stamping me without even looking. All I had to worry about was whether or not Bitch-face would notice that I had this new entry stamp.

My papers had arrived while we were gone and I sent them off at once to Barcelona to be officially translated. Once I had all my papers in order, I made my journey back to the police station. I wanted to give the impression that I was someone worthy of Spanish residency, so I dressed nice in a long, fitted green dress and let my long blonde hair out of it usual prison of a tight bun. Fernando always says that I look nicer with my hair down, so I decided to go with a Spaniard's advice. The line was much longer this time, not only trickling down the stairs, but out the door and wrapping around the block. Good thing I had brought a book. As I went to pull out my book, the girl in front of me told me to go check in at the desk because she thought she was the last of the line for today and that they were giving out numbers for the next day.

I went to the front desk and, from a distance, I could tell that Fernando was not the only man who liked my hair down. I was greeted by a huge smile. I smiled back and told the receptionist that I was not sure if I should wait in line or get a number for the following day.

"German, are you?"

"No," I hardly got out before he took his next guess.

"Swedish?"

I told him that actually my ancestors were Swedish; however, I was from the USA. He seemed to like this response. He asked me what it was I needed and I said that I just had to turn in my paperwork to apply for residency.

"Go up and see Jesús on the second floor. Tell him Jose sent you."

"But last time I went to the first floor?"

He assured me that where I needed to go was the second floor and that there was no line there. I walked past all of the people waiting on the stairwell. I felt ridiculously over dressed and out of place. I was about a good six inches taller than everyone in the line and my loose blonde hair that reached my waist stood out against all the black hair as much as a fire walking up the stairs would have. Many women in line had babies wailing in their arms and some mothers had spit-up on their shoulders.

Having traveled through South America for some time, I was reasonably sure by the accents I was hearing as I walked past that the majority, if not all the people in line, were from either Peru or Ecuador. Some were not even speaking Spanish. I thought I recognized a bit of Quechua.

I remembered how surprised Fernando and I had been on a bus in Peru when we realized we were the only people speaking Spanish. We had no idea the ancient Inca language was still so alive. An elderly lady sitting next to me had tried to teach me a few words on a long bus ride. I am not sure if it had to do with the language being very difficult to pronounce, the fact that she had no teeth, or the wads of coco leaves she had packed into her cheeks, but I learned not one word of Quechua on my trip apart from Machu Picchu which, despite what the guides said about 'old peak' over the four days of climbing, I am convinced means 'mountain of no air', or 'mountain of people with three hearts and ten lungs'.

As I passed the people in line, I was glad that they would not receive any false hope from Bitch-face. Nothing is worse than overly cheery people giving you false hope so they feel good that they made you feel good, not worrying about your outcome once you are out of their view. I could never do Bitch-face's job well. I am a giver of false hope. I cannot stand to see people despair and will do anything to avoid people despairing in my presence.

I reached the second floor and found a closed door. I looked around. Nothing suggested what I should do next, so I knocked.

"*Entra; entra,*" a deep voice bellowed from within.

As I walked in, a bald man in his late fifties stood up from his leather chair behind his desk and said, "Argentina."

I assumed that this was a guess at my nationality and was flattered because of the amazingly beautiful women I had seen on my recent visit to Argentina. He seemed like a flirtatious and fun guy, so I smiled and shook my head, not giving my accent away by speaking. He looked me over and his eyes stopped around the middle of my body (where my narrow waste and large ass are located, their dimensions very obvious thanks to my knit dress that I had thought this morning made me look classy) and said, "Brazil."

I know from listening to drunken conversations that many Spanish men think that all Brazilian women are endowed with many enticing qualities, narrow waist and large juicy ass being a few.

I was beginning to get a bit worried at where this was going and that maybe this Jesús guy had a few of his own boxes to check in what was necessary in order to apply for residency, so I blurted out, "I am from the United States of America and am here to turn in my paperwork and apply for residency via my Spanish husband."

He made a *give-me* gesture for my paperwork (which was strikingly similar to a *come-hither* gesture) and began to peruse my documents.

"What you need to do is take this down and turn it in on the first floor."

'No shit' almost jumped out of my mouth, but I was able to say instead, "I thought so, but Jose said to come up here and see you."

At this, he smiled a big, knowing smile and, with all my paperwork still in his hands, said, "Follow me."

By the time I realized where we were going, it was too late to stop him. I would have preferred to have been taken to a secret room in his office or a supply closet to perform extra necessary requirements not previously checked on my paper than to where I realized he was taking me.

"No, no," I said as Jesús reached for the door knob to Bitch-face's office. "I will come back tomorrow. I... I... I'm really in a big hurry anyway."

He gave me *a* 'knock off all this nonsense' look, and walked into the office while the line that went on to affinity looked at us with curious, not yet angry stares. He had all my hard-to-get-again paperwork in his hands, so I did not have much of an option and followed him. Luckily, Bitch-face was just finishing up with the woman in the office, so the breach of confidentiality that I was imposing was not as bad as it could have been. As the woman left the office, Bitch-face focused her laser beams on me while listening to Jesús. I could see in her eyes, given the current situation, she did not take my dress and loose, long blonde hair as an attempt to look nice and classy, but rather as a tactic that attractive women use to get men to do things for them like cut in line instead of getting a number the way that everyone else has to do. Not being an overly attractive woman, she had no conspiratorial feeling for what she thought I was doing. Pure annoyance radiated from her being as Jesús explained that I just needed to turn in this paperwork, but had accidentally gone to his office instead. Great. Now I was not only a conniving bitch that uses her physical assets to get what she wants, but a freaking idiot to top it off.

No one else had walked into the office, so I assumed that everyone in line knew that I had effectively cut in line and took the next turn. I wanted to die. Bitch-face let one of her very uncomfortable silences fall (so long that tumbleweeds actually did begin to blow across the floor this time) then thrust her hand towards Jesús for my paperwork (no *come-hither* gesture about it) and began to roughly go through my paperwork. Jesús gave me a conspiring smile and booked it on out of there before he could be vaporized.

After she was satisfied that all of my paperwork was as it should be, she shuffled me over to a table, shoved my thumb onto an ink pad and then smashed it against a paper that had my two passport photos attached and told me to sign in the box above my thumbprint. "If they accept your application, you should have your residency card within three months." She handed me an official-looking paper and said, "This is your temporary residency for three months until you are notified otherwise."

She gave me a disapproving look, which I understood to be my dismissal. With my head hung in shame, I thanked her and was out of there. No one in line said anything to me as I passed and I had no idea if I was getting dirty looks, because I kept my head down until I reached my car.

When I arrived home, I told Fernando my shameful story. He just laughed and said, "Welcome to Spain."

Before three months were up, an official-looking letter arrived for me. I ripped it open and was delighted when a card fell out onto the table and not a piece of paper with a rejection that I so justly deserved. I was now a Spanish resident! I was no longer an illegal immigrant! I was very happy with my residency card until I flipped it over.

"What the fuck?" was out of my mouth before I even realized it.

From the kitchen, Fernando chirped, "What?"

"Something that you are going to like very much."

He came over to inspect my residency card. He looked over the front and gave me an 'and?' look.

"Flip it over."

He did as he was told and burst into a laughing fit. "It's like you're my little pet. You better be good because I have the power to throw you out of this country if you misbehave," he barely managed between gales of laughter.

I shot him the nastiest look I was capable of. '*Vinculado a Fernando*...' is what it said on the back of my residency card, along with his ID number. I was pretty sure that I knew what *vinculado* meant, but wanted to double check before throwing a fit. I opened up my computer and typed *vinculado* into my Spanish-English dictionary. Linked to. Tied to. Bonded to. I was tied to Fernando. I was not good enough to be my own person; I had to be linked to someone else. Fernando was in ecstasy. He had somehow interpreted this as Spain saying that I belonged to him while here. Every dinner party we attended afterwards, either I with indignation or Fernando, out of sheer amusement, passed my residency card around the table. It is always a source of great hilarity. The little no-bra-wearing, green, feminist, politically correct, North American belonging to a Spaniard.

I did not realize the flip side of this until Fernando sent me to buy something urgent for the museum at *Gros Mercat*, a wholesale warehouse that only sells to businesses. I went to pay and handed Fernando's *Gros Mercat* card over. The cashier informed me that I was not on the account and, therefore, could not buy there with this card. "But I am his wife," I pleaded, knowing that Fernando was out excavating in the field with no phone coverage to confirm that I could, indeed, make this urgent purchase with his card.

"Do you have any way to prove that?" the cashier asked.

I hung my head in defeat. "No, but it is really urgen... wait, I do have proof!" I pulled out my residency card and showed the front and back sides to her. "Can you believe how *machista* that is?" I asked, giving her a conspiratorial smile that suggested what we poor women have to put up with just for being women. I hoped it did not occur to her that all immigrants had this on the back of their residency cards, not just women. She raised her eyebrows in a knowing way while nodding her head and swiped the card.

I came to find out that this little song and dance worked as well with Fernando's credit cards. Menorcans respect matrimony very much. So much so that I was able to buy a whole new outfit plus shoes and earrings that day.

* * * *

Residency cards via matrimony are valid for five years and are renewable, granted that the immigrant in question is still married to a Spaniard. Therefore, I never really thought too seriously about taking the next step to citizenship, which I was entitled to after one year of marriage and residency. Many of my friends from South America have dual citizenship; however, I was under the impression that the USA did not allow dual citizenship. You're with us or you're not. I believe that in the past it was this way because I have spoken to Americans who had to forfeit their US citizenship when taking on a new citizenship. But, after snooping around on the internet, it looks like now it is strongly advised that you do not take on a second citizenship, but does not mention anything to the effect of you forfeiting your US citizenship if you do.

Spanish citizenship was something that was becoming more and more attractive. At first, the difference between residency and citizenship did not bother me in the least. I was content enough that I was now legally residing in Spain and that I could be legally employed. However, little incidences started to accumulate, making me feel more and more an outsider to this world I had decided to live in. Nothing big... but the little things started adding up and began gnawing at me.

Fernando and I were on a repeat visit to Argentina and were on a very limited budget. Even so, our Argentinean friends had convinced us that we had to travel with them to Chile. We began making plans and everyone was excited about our trip until I found out that I would have to pay $100 on entry of Chile with my North American passport. No one else had to pay an entry fee. This was $100 that I did not have. Even though I encouraged everyone else to go on without me, the trip was cancelled and everyone stayed home because of the non-Spaniard. There was talk about going to Brazil instead, but that was quickly vetoed when we found out that I would also have to pay $100 on entry to Brazil.

Later, it was explained to me that Chile and Brazil impose this entry or visa fee as a way of getting even with the United States. People from Chile, Brazil and Argentina have to pay $100 to obtain an interview for consideration of being permitted entrance to the USA.

"There is no guarantee with this interview." Carol, who was explaining this to me over a dinner that I had prepared, lost $300 dollars (which is three times as much in Argentina currency). She wanted to show her two little boys Disney World, Washington D.C. and New York. She paid and obtained an interview and prepared extensively for it. Basically, they just want to know that you will not stay in the USA. She had a folder with documents proving that she had her own business, two separate bank accounts (one personal and one for her business) that's sum was over $10,000 (no small feat in Argentina), a house, two cars and a husband who was running the business in her absence. Very good reasons not to stay in the USA and return to Argentina.

She went to her interview full of confidence, folder in hand. Her interview consisted of a man in a booth looking at her passport for a moment, stamping a 'denied' on it and asking her to move aside so he could help the next person in line. She asked him to please look at her folder. He told her there was no need. Women between the ages of thirty and forty were more statically likely to stay in the USA. She could petition for an interview again after the date on the stamp in her passport. Five years later. He then told her again to move aside so that he could help the next person in line.

Though Carol was nice and I felt that she liked me, she thought it wonderful that Brazil and Chile charged US citizens to enter their country and hoped that Argentina would do the same in the near future. "You should not complain; at least you have the guarantee of entering when you pay your money."

I knew she was right and I did agree with her, but I was still annoyed that I had given her the best cut of meat from the *asado*.

After our failed travel plans, our friends jokingly call me the non-Spaniard until we left. I had promised them that next year I would come with my citizenship and we would go to both Chile and Brazil (we had decided that we would have to come every year after our friends made Fernando godfather of their daughter born while we were there).

My husband promised that he was not upset that we could not travel to Chile or Brazil... He had thought that was the source of my gloomy mood. What was really bothering me was that I was feeling definitely non-Spanish as we headed back to Spain. That was the first occurrence that made me aware of my resident status, of the difference between my husband and me because of a little booklet of paper. On the way back to Spain (and every time we traveled outside of Europe), Fernando and I were separated at passport control and he had to wait for almost an hour for me to come through the foreigner line. The passport control official spoke to me in English even though I handed him my Spanish residency card along with my passport and answered all of his questions in Spanish. I am sure he did this to be courteous, but already being sensitive, I felt wounded, taking it as a rejection of me as one of them.

In Barcelona, we had to recheck in because it was cheaper to book a flight from Barcelona to Menorca separately than flying straight to Menorca. We both handed over our identification cards and the man attending us at the check-in counter suck in air, signaling us for something unpleasant, and said to me, "I am sorry, but you have to buy a new ticket."

"What?" I shouted in outrage. "I bought the ticket at the same time as my husband and with the same credit card."

"Yes, but you put down that you were entitled to the Balearic Islands resident discount."

"Yes, because I AM a resident of the Balearic Island; can you not see that on my identification card? It just so happens that I have the same address as my husband."

"Yes, *señora*, I see that; however, I also see that you are from the USA."

"Um... yes," I said, having no idea where he was going with this.

"The Balearic resident discount is only for people born within the European community."

"That is crap. I have flown many times with this discount as I *am* a Balearic resident!"

"Yes, well now we have been forced to enforce this law. I would get into trouble if I did not. Your name was in red, signaling me that I had to check and enter in your nationality."

"This is absurd. Whatever… so what, can I just pay you the forty percent discount that was given to me?"

"I am sorry *señora*, but you have to buy a new ticket."

"What! This is un believable."

"Sorry, you should have checked the terms and conditions of residency."

"What the hell. On the webpage it asked me if I am a Balearic resident. I checked the box because I *am* a Balearic resident. I pay taxes in Baleares, I volunteer in the Baleares… I AM a resident of the Balearic Island."

"I don't doubt that, *señora*; however, you were not born within the European community, which makes you un-eligible for this discount."

"Well why the hell can't I just pay the difference?"

"Because that would encourage people to try every time, and we just can't have that. If you go over to the ticket booth, I am sure they can find a reasonable-priced ticket for you."

"This is discriminatory! If you are a resident in the Balearic Islands, you should be entailed to the forty percent Balearic resident discount. It should not matter where you were born."

"Sorry, *señora*, you are more than welcome to file a complaint form if you would like."

Torn between jumping over the counter and severely maiming the man or buying a new ticket while voicing my outrage, I chose the more sensible of the two and paid a fortune for a one-way ticket from Barcelona to Menorca leaving in two hours.

Becoming a citizen was becoming more and more appealing. With a Spanish passport, this would not happen. All of the advantages of becoming a full citizen started to parade through my mind: I would no longer be *vinculado* to anyone. I would be allowed to stay and work in Spain (and Europe) without the condition of being married if that ever became an issue. I would not have to worry about renewing. I would be able to use the quick European Union line when going through passport control. I would receive the Balearic resident discount. I would be able to travel to countries free of charge that I would otherwise have to pay $100 to get into using my North American passport. And, even though it sounds ridiculous, it just seems cool to have more than one passport.

I went back to the police station and asked about how to petition for citizenship. Luckily, there was no line and the man at the desk (not Jose) had a paper that listed all of the necessary paperwork for citizenship. However, I had to deal with that at the *Registro Civil*, because the office at the police station only dealt with residency. I would only have to come back to the police station once all of my paperwork had been approved by the *Registro Civil* to do an interview with Jesús on the second floor. Fantastic... at least I knew how to dress for the interview. I wrote down the directions for the *Registo Civil* that the man at the desk gave me and went home to see what I needed in order to petition for citizenship.

After a few months, I had all of the paperwork that I needed and headed on my way. The line was much more reasonable than at the police station. When my turn came, I walked up to the counter and told the man, who was around my age, that I was here to turn in my paperwork and apply for citizenship. I handed over my papers. He looked over them for a few minutes, then informed me that I could not apply for citizenship because I was not married... in Spain, anyways. This came as a shock because I had understood (or convinced myself anyways) that when I turned in my marriage certificate, which had been sent to the Secretary of State attaining the Apostille making it valid here in Europe, and having it officially translated, when petitioning for my residency that they had verified my marriage here, therefore, giving me my residency.

However, this turned out not to be the case. It turns out that the institution that gives you your residency is completely separate from the institution that confirms marriage and gives you your citizenship, even though you need to have your residency in order to gain your citizenship. So following my line of reasoning, one can imagine my surprise when they informed me that I was not married here. Well, being that I had all of my papers anyway (marriage certificate, birth certificate, criminal history record.... all passed through the secretary of state with their Apostille in array with the *Convention de La Haye du 5 octobre 1961* and officially translated, proof of cohabitation, proof of living in Es Migjorn Gran, a copy of Fernando's Spanish ID card, a copy of my Spanish ID card and Fernando's birth certificate, which his dad had to stand in line for hours for), I decided to make the most out of the situation and asked if I could go ahead with the process of making our marriage legal here in Spain. He said yes, but that it would take about a year and when I received that, along with something called a family book, then I could apply for citizenship. I said great and started handing over the necessary papers. While I was handing over the papers, I asked if I had to turn in the originals and he said yes. I asked if I would have to do the same when asking for my citizenship in a year's time. He said yes. Just to make sure I was understanding correctly, I asked, "So I had to turn in the originals to get my residency. Now I have to turn in again the originals for confirming my marriage. And I will have to turn in originals when I petition my citizenship.... all originals, all with an Apostille and all officially translated. Three times. Correct?"

He started talking to me in English at this point, which I could not understand. I told him that I understood Spanish perfectly; it was just the system that I could not grasp. He apologized and I told him that it was not his fault because he was really nice and trying to help.

I had almost sorted out all of the papers that he needed when he saw the confirmation paper of where I was living. When he saw this, he seemed to melt and set his forehead on the counter. He then asked the counter if my husband also lived in Es Migjorn Gran and I said yes and shuffled through the papers until I came upon the paper of proof of cohabitation, which, of course, is in Es Migjon Gran. He still had his forehead against the counter when I asked if it was a bad thing to live in Es Migjorn Gran.

He answered, "Today it is, because Es Migjorn Grand corresponds to the *Registro Civil* in Ciutadella and not Mahón on these types of things. They close at midday and you won't make it in time today."

I kept all of the evil things that I was going to say about Spain under control and cheerfully said, "Well, at least I have all of the paperwork done."

He raised his head from the counter and said, "It may not be the same."

To this, I thought I might go postal. I was about ready to explode and tell everyone in the office that this was my first day off in three months and that I did not have time for such inefficiency. However, I smiled instead and said, "Well at least I hope it is similar. Thank you for all of your help and sorry for being such a bother."

He assured me that I had not been a bother and wished me luck. The other woman working behind the counter yelled after me, "You're not married here, sweetie, but it is easy to fix; it just takes a long time."

"No problem," I answered. "If it is easy to fix, I am happy. That it takes a long time is not important because I am married to my husband for life."

This made her smile and I waved as I walked out the door. What I really wanted to say was, 'fuck, now that I will not be receiving my Spanish passport this year, I will have to pay $100 to get into Chile and another $100 if I want to go to Brazil with my North American passport'. But I imagine that having to pay to get into other countries is not an excuse for getting my Spanish passport that would have gained me much sympathy, so I said it in my head and broke out in hives.

11

Simple, Good Food

Elegance is often just simplicity in its perfection. Most Menorcan dishes are just that, simple and elegant, letting each unique flavor express its own excellence, without tampering it. I have often thought this approach to gastronomy is in part responsible for the longevity so common on the island. Simple, good food.

Being completely surrounded by the sea has its advantages, the most important being fresh seafood year round. This fact allows me to amaze and dazzle my guest regardless of the fact that most six year olds have more culinary skills than I do. Luckily, the sea creatures that end up on my table do most of the work for me and allow me to take all of the credit.

My favorite way to start off a meal is with shellfish for various reasons... quick, easy and tasty. The mussels on the island are small and delicious. I am not a great connoisseur of gastronomy, but I have caught waiters selling me *Menorcan mussels,* only to have them put a steaming pot of large, plump mussels in front of me. Yes, very tasty, but not small *Menorcan mussels.* I buy my mussels (and all other products of the sea) from a little fishermen's co-op in Ferreries, the neighboring town of Es Migjorn Gran (the same people that bring the fish market to Es Migjorn Gran three times a week). The men do the fishing and the women do the selling. Both seem to take their work quite seriously and are truly concerned with customer satisfaction. I once made a comment that a few of the mussels I had previously bought were open and I had thrown them out. I was really just wanting to know if what I had done was correct, and I guess it was, because the woman selling gave me an extra kilo of mussels that day to make up for the three that were inedible. I felt extremely guilty and she must have seen how I felt because she smiled and told me that, if I continued on with 'that face', she was going to give me another kilo for spite.

It was to these women that I confessed one day that I had no idea what to do with anything from the sea, or anything edible, for that matter.

"Well, if you have no idea how to cook, then the sea is a good place to start because you can make your husband happy by just putting fish in the oven and grilling or steaming shellfish."

My first thought was that I was just as eager to please myself as I was to please my husband, but I decided to keep that part of my internal monolog internal and opened my ears as how to please my husband via easy to prepare seafood.

"To start off, I recommend a dish of one of four different types of easy and cheap shellfish: steamed mussels, grilled razor clams, grilled cockles, and grilled clams."

I was shown an example of each and commented that cockles looked like normal clams to me. After looks of disdain, I was told that, apart from many other differences, cockles were smaller and tastier than clams. Mussels, I was told, would need to be cleaned first, pulling out all of the seaweed between the clamped-shut shells. The next step

was putting a few fingers[8] of water in a pot and adding
cracked pepper, laurel leaves and lemon juice to the water.
I was then to place my metal steamer that I used for
steaming vegetables on top of the bit of water, add the
mussels, put the lid on, turn the heat up and let the water
boil for a few minutes until the mussels opened. Once they
had opened, they were ready to eat after a squeeze of lemon
on top. Perfect. Even I could handle that.

Cockles, razor clams, and clams turned out to be as
easy as mussels, but without the cleaning. All I had to do
was put some olive oil in a pan, and chop up some fresh
parsley, and a bit of garlic. Throw that into the hot olive oil
along with the above-mentioned shellfish (a splash of white
wine being optional), cover with a lid and wait a few
minutes until they opened, which meant that they were
ready to eat. As with mussels, give them a squeeze of fresh
lemon once they open.

One of the fish ladies confided in me her secret to
perfect razor clams. "My husband loves gilled razor clams,
but he hates it when he crunches sand between his teeth,
which often happens with these yummy critters. My trick is
to buy them fresh and alive, the only real way to buy
shellfish, and put them in saltwater for an entire day before
cooking them. They will spit out the sand this way. Once
they are done spitting out sand, throw those babies in hot
oil!"

My animal-loving vegetarian friend told me when I
teased her about eating mussels that she ate anything that
did not blink. I decided to take the same approach when

---

[8] Spaniards measure small amounts in fingers… the size of a fingertip
horizontal. For example, if someone is making an alcoholic beverage
and asks how much of the given alcohol you want in it, a common
response would be, 'two or three fingers'.

painfully killing them... If it didn't blink, I could throw it alive in hot oil.

With my new hypocritical reasoning in place, I thought, *wow, how easy to cook!* I had four very nice options for the first course and decided on mussels. I still had the second course to deal with and asked for help.

"There are many good fish that you can just throw in the oven, but let's just start off with a few. *Dorada* (gilt-head) and *Lubina* (sea bass) are nice white fish that are relatively cheap and one small fish per person is usually perfect. You need to tell the fish lady that you want to cook them in the oven and they will know what to do."

I wondered what they were going to do to the fish and she explained that any fish going in the oven just needed to be gutted and scaled.

"And the head?"

This caused peals of laughter. "Head and all, dear. You will see how your husband likes it. You can stuff some lemon slices in the belly where it was gutted, sprinkle lemon juice, olive oil and salt on it and leave it until its skin looks crispy and bubbly."

"So I just basically throw the fish on the baking sheet, head and all, and leave it in the oven?"

"Yeap... and while it is baking, you can start a load of laundry, bathe the kids, take a shower and set the table."

I bitterly thought, *yeah right,* feeling like a complete domestic failure. God, I hope that Fernando's previous girlfriend was as domestically challenged as I am so that he would not notice my deficiency. I decided that, if he ever pointed it out, I would attack him on not having learned English yet. No, I do not play fair and yes, I know I am going to Hell.

The steamed mussels and the oven-baked fish (I decided on *dorada*), head and all, were a huge success and Fernando even hugged me in congratulations on not just my meal, which he knew was an amazing feat in itself for me, but also on socializing with locals and becoming more involved. I basked in his compliments and understood why the fish ladies were so keen on pleasing their husbands.

When Christmas rolled around, the fish ladies told me that I had to prepare grilled *langostinos*, which was a typical dish at Christmas time. It seemed odd to me that grilled king prawns were a Christmas dish, but I had no complaints. I was told to heat a bit of olive oil in a pan. Once it was really hot, add in the prawns and give them a generous sprinkling of salt. "Sea salt with large crystals," the fish ladies advised.

After a minute or two, flip them over and give another sprinkling of salt and wait another minute or two. A squeeze of lemon juice and presto. I looked at the prawns that seemed to be wearing a non-edible outer protection. When I inquired about how to eat them, the fish ladies just laughed and told me that my husband could surely show me. However, they did suggest that I prepare little bowls of water with lemon wedges in them to clean fingers in afterwards.

I prepared our little finger-washing bowls and grilled the *langostinos.* When we sat down engulfed in the wonderful smells of rich seafood, I asked my husband how we were going to eat these things. Fernando, always loving to be the professor, put on his lecture face and began to explain, "In certain situations, the most proper way would be to use knife and fork, first cutting off the legs, then peeling the shell. However, this is not easy to do and you lose the best part, which is sucking the juices." He picked up a *langostino* and I followed suit. "First, suck the body."

Following along, I sucked the outer transparent shell.

"Then you break the head from the body, trying not to let any juices spill. The best part is sucking the juice out of the head. Suck the head until no juices are left inside,"

Fernando commanded. I must have not sufficiently sucked because Fernando again commanded, "Suck; suck; suck; it's the best part!"

I now understood why the fish ladies thought it would be funny to have my husband explain about how to eat *langostinos*… I am sure they knew about the sucking and sucking, especially of the head. After I had assured Fernando that I had thoroughly sucked the head, we proceeded to the next step. "Pull the legs off. Once you pull the legs off, it is easier to peal the shell."

Once the legs and shell were removed, only perfect pinkish-white meat was left. I eagerly sucked my next victims and, when I finished with the bunch, I sucked the rich juices from my fingers, much to the offense of my husband's proper European table etiquette, having completely forgotten about the little bowls of water with lemon wedges.

There are other offerings from the sea that I thoroughly enjoy, but have decided not to lower my self-esteem in attempting to prepare them because they can easily be great or chewy and horrible; octopus and fried baby squid. I have been told that octopus needs to either be frozen or beaten in order to break up the fibers it has. If this is not done, very chewy results are the consequence. However, this is often the case even if the proper octopus-preparing techniques are followed. I do not prepare octopus, but oh do I love to eat it. My favorite style of octopus is *pulpo a la Gallega*, Galician style. It is thinly sliced, boiled, and served over-boiled potatoes dribbled with olive oil and sprinkled with red, half sweet, half spicy pepper. If it is chewy, it is horrible, but when it is soft in the mouth like a ripe fruit, it is an amazing, mouth-watering dish. I never thought that I would eat octopus, but now I know I could not live without it.

Chipirones, fried baby squid, are a very common *tapa.*[9] They may not be the most environmentally conscience choice, but wow are they good with a beer or *xandy.*[10] Basically, it is the entire baby squid battered and fried. Amazing. When my childhood best friend's four-year-old daughter came to visit me for two weeks, she happily deemed them 'Menorcan French fries'.

* * * *

The sea is not my only provider of gastronomic pleasure on Menorca. I could not face the possibility of life without Menorcan cheese. Menorcan cheese has almost cost me my

---

[9] I would like to clarify *tapas,* which are as stereotypical of Spain as *sangria* and *flamenco* dancing. Many people ask for *tapas* as if it was a specific thing. Certain places may have specialty *tapas.* However, *tapas* are kind of like snacks… little dishes of different things that usually friends order and eat between them while drinking a beer, wine, etc. It would be like ordering a bunch of starters or appetizers and sharing it between friends and loved ones. Spaniards don't usually eat until around 9 to 10 pm and *tapas* usually fill the space between lunch and dinner. In places like Granada (extremely famous for the concept of *tapas*), you get a free *tapa* with each drink you order. The first free *tapa* is always the largest and then gets progressively smaller with each drink. So if you are on a budget while in Granada (but do not want to sacrifice alcohol and socializing) it is best to go to a bar, have a drink, eat your free first *tapa* and then proceed to the next bar to repeat the process. I visited Granada for one week and never had to buy food (forget the fact that I was buzzed the entire time).

[10] *Xandy* or chandy is beer with lemon soda added in to it. It may sound strange, but it is extremely refreshing on hot days. This beverage, when called a *clara,* usually means that normal soda should be used instead of lemon soda. However, this is not always the case, so it is best to clarify when ordering… I.e. '*Xandy* with lemon please'. In Tarragona, a *Xandy* is called *shampoo,* while in certain parts of the Basque country it is called bleach (*lejia*). I found this all out the hard way while working in the museum's bar.

life on various occasions, but I love it all the same. Some smaller farms produce their own cheese; however, there are four or five names that dominate the cheese industry here and they sometimes buy milk from other farms for their cheese production.

I do not wake up easily in the morning and consequently do not react quickly until a nice thick espresso with a wee bit of milk has been ingested. I have this necessary stimulant at the museum, so on the half an hour drive along the curvy and winding country roads from Es Migjorn Gran to Cavalleria, one could say I am not at my best. While in this groggy, hating the world state, I have almost been obliterated after a sharp curve by extremely large trucks that drive out to the remote farms on the island to collect milk. My first reaction to this situation was to say every single curse word I knew in both English and in Spanish, followed by my second reaction, which was to swerve too hard in the opposite direction and scrape the entire side of my car along a rock wall that line small country roads. Luckily, Fernando did not see the scrape until later on in the evening, so I was able to blame it on a 'stupid tourist' who must have scraped my car while it was parked in the museum's parking lot.

After I realized that the milk-gathering man and his huge frigging truck used the narrow country road at the same time I did every day, I decided to have my espresso at the bar next to my house before journeying off to work. Now the milk-gathering man and I are great friends, waving enthusiastically to each other every morning.

I have tried many different local cheeses at local gastronomy fairs and I always choose the same farm as my favorite cheese maker, Subaida in the town of Alaior. I decided that I would drive out to the farm and buy my cheese there, which seemed to me much more authentic than buying it at the supermarket, which has a section dedicated to local cheese. The farm is located on the outskirts of Alaior and I was pleased at how easy it was to find. I drove down a long dirt driveway and parked before I was actually in the barnyard. I was not sure where to go and I was the only person there, so I walked past cows eating towards the nicest barn-like structure hoping that would be the place where I could buy cheese. I rounded the corner and was in Heaven. I was in a cheese-producing warehouse. At the far end was a counter and below it in a glass case were all of the different types of cheese that they make ready for tasting. Once I reached the counter, a woman asked if I would like to sample different cheeses. *Oh what a silly question,* I thought… could she not see my drool?

I like strong, hard cheese. For sampling, they had out soft cheese, semi-cured cheese, cured cheese and another type that I did not recognize. I asked the woman if I could try the cured cheese, which I thought was the strongest and hardest. The woman watched while I enjoyed and asked if I had ever tried the *añejo* cheese. That was the other type of cheese that I had seen in the case. I had never tried it. She handed me a slice and explained, "The *añejo* is the strongest cheese we have. Our cured cheese is aged for over five months, where *añejo* is aged for over ten."

What an astounding and perfect concept, I thought as my neck began to sweat from the strength of the cheese. I had a new love. I ordered half a kilo of *añejo* and happily walked back to my car. On the way home, I splurged on a good bottle of red wine to accompany my cheese later on that night.

It was my day off, but it was August and I thought I would go see how the museum was handling the ridiculous amounts of tourists who conspire to make our life hell by all coming during the same month. Fernando looked like he had been run over by a rototiller and I told him to go home and that I would help the others close up. He nodded his head and puckered his lips in an attempt to blow me a kiss, but was too tired to complete the motion, grabbed his car keys and walked out dragging his feet.

I helped close up and felt good about my day off. I had slept in late, found the most perfect cheese on the planet and saved my husband from death via heat and tourist. I parked my car and walked up to my house, eagerly anticipating my cheese and wine. My happiness ended quickly when I saw Fernando's dark expression. I tried to think of anything that I had recently done that would anger him, and came up blank, so I asked, "What's wrong?"

"Could you please tell me what dead thing is in the refrigerator? It smells so bad that I will not even try to open it again until whatever it is that is in there is out."

In my perfect-cheese bliss, I had completely forgotten that Fernando hates cheese more than anything. He hates everything about it, its texture, its color, and most of all its smell. Shit. What was I going to do with my cheese? I should have let the heat and tourists finish Fernando in. He must have seen in my face that I was more for my cheese than for his life because he compromised, saying that I could keep my cheese, but only in a very sealed Tupperware and that I had to warn him when I was going to open it so he could stay out of the kitchen. At least he now knows where he stands when it come to my Menorcan cheese.

* * * *

Menorcan gastronomical bliss also comes directly from the earth. Summer brings with it fruits and vegetables and eating outside on the terrace at nighttime by candlelight. One of my favorite gifts of summer are figs. My summer evening walks along dirt roads are perfumed with the rejuvenating smell of fig. There are many fig trees on Menorca and many types of figs. My favorite is the *figaflor*, which bears fruit at the end of June. These are usually the largest, sweetest and juiciest. Once those are finished, I am saved by the *agostenques*, the figs that ripen in August. And just when I dread that fig season is over, there is one last gift, the fig trees that give us sweet fruit in October.

I eat figs plain for breakfast, as a midday snack, as a hold-me-over from when I arrive home from work starving until I get dinner done, and for dessert. I also sometimes even make them part of my dinner. When it is too hot to eat anything warm, the most refreshing course imaginable is slices of very ripe tomato with generous slices of fresh buffalo mozzarella placed on the tomatoes, topped with slices of ripe, juicy figs, all dribbled with honey produced by happy Menorcan bees.

There is a very typical Menorcan dessert, which is easy enough even for me to attempt called 'figs in the oven'. Very few ingredients are required: 500 grams of figs, 4 tbsp of sugar, 1 dl water. Turn the oven to 180 (Celsius). While the oven heats up, cut the tips off the figs. Pour the water into a clay pot (living in Menorca means you must own a clay cooking pot because over half of the recipes of the island require one). Place yummy figs into water and clay pot, sprinkle them with sugar and bake for 30 minutes. Let it cool and serve warm.

* * * *

Many locals on the island have a *huerta*, a small patch of land that they use for gardening. These little plots usually have a small, whitewashed building that looks like a mini house. This is where all the gardening supplies and produce are kept. *Huertas* are usually on the outskirts of each town.

Luckily, my neighbor downstairs has one. She also has a spare key to my house. This has turned out to be a great combination because I come home and often find a bag of fresh veggies in my doorway. She also has a patch of land behind her apartment, which is below my window. From this patch of land grows the most amazing lemon tree on Menorca. It bursts yellow and its branches hang with its burden of fruit. When I look at it from my window, I often think of a cow with a full udder, badly in need of milking. Paula and I have often spent afternoons contemplating the best way to pillage the tree from our window. We justify our devious plans as compensation for having to listen to her. Her normal speaking voice is similar to a foghorn and she starts talking around 6 am. If her husband is not home to yell at, she talks to her cat. The stupid thing answers all of her bellowing with a meow, encouraging her to continue. We further justify our lemon-pillaging scheme because of her small and very active canary that she keeps in shamelessly tiny cage, which hangs in our communal light patio (all of our kitchen's windows face each other separated by an interior patio that only the pharmacy below has access to). Paula and I can't stand to see animals in small cages and have spent even more afternoons thinking about how to free the bird than how to pillage the lemon tree.

One day when Paula had her head out the window contemplating the canary's breakout, she asked me if I had hung my underwear up near the window so they would dry faster. I was amazed because that is exactly what I had done and I asked her how she could possibly know this because I had already put them away.

"Because there are panties on the patio floor."

I was not too eager to ask the pharmacist passage for my panties, and even less so when I saw which ones they were... They were, of course, my red satin g-strings.

Days passed and I had completely forgotten about my panties until the neighbor left me a bag of veggies in my doorway (making me feel guilty about our previous scheming). I opened it up and found two eggplants, a head of lettuce and my red g-strings. I wondered how she had come upon my panties being that the only access to the interior patio was through the pharmacy, but was happy enough because now I could make stuffed eggplant for dinner.

Later on when I went to the pharmacy to gossip with Carmen, she told me that there was a communal cleaning of the interior patio (I had missed it because I was working that Sunday) and my foghorn neighbor below, announced to everyone that the red satin g-sting panties were the Yankee's and that she would give them back to me. I have no idea how she knew this, but no one had questioned her knowledge of my undergarments.

Fresh fruits, vegetables and the most amazing lemon tree in existence are not the only gifts of the land that my neighbor reaps. One day, Nicolas was over for a dinner. Fernando and I do not smoke, but know that Nicolas will die within sixteen minutes without his nicotine fix, so we agreed to let him smoke in the house as long as he did it out the window. While I was finishing up dinner, I heard Nicolas exclaim, "*Ostia puta*, your neighbor has five marijuana plants growing in her back yard!"

I could not believe that this old, gossipy woman had five plants of marijuana growing in her back yard and went to check. Sure enough, there were five huge marijuana plants in plain sight for all of the neighbors to see. Fernando, Nicolas and I all had the same thought: it is one of her shady kids. Poor thing, she would be so embarrassed if she knew. Fernando decided to go down and give her the horrible news that her kids had planted five illegal plants in her yard. When Fernando told her, she said, "I know; I make some really great tea with them."

Yeah right.

The next day, I went to the pharmacy to share this juicy bit of gossip and, while Carmen and I laughed, Lucas looked wounded and said, "I never get any marijuana tea in the bags of vegetables she gives me."

This made Carmen and me laugh even harder.

I told him, "Don't worry, neither do I, but I do get red g-string panties in mine." Then I proceeded to tell them how my panties had been delivered back to me.

*　*　*　*

Embutidos. The translation of 'cold meats' does not do them justice. There are many different types of cold meats, but my favorites are *jamón serrano*, *sobrassada*, and *carnixulla*.

My friend, Anna, with whom I had waitressed while putting myself through university, went to Spain while I was still contemplating going there. When she came back, I excitedly asked her opinion of Spain. "Spanish bars and supermarkets are disgusting. They are full of pigs' legs hanging from the roof." This was the first thing she told me about Spain.

I had no way to understand this. I imagined bloody, severed legs hanging from roof beams and could not believe it. When I finally arrived in Spain myself, I almost died from a laughing fit when I realized what she was talking about, *jamón serrano*, or Spanish ham. I find it utterly amazing how a cured leg of pig can taste so good.

When someone from the States says 'let's buy a ham', one thinks of something that you are going to pop in the oven and have a feast with. When a Spaniard says 'let's buy a ham', it is a cured pig's leg perfect for eating at any time of the day. A *jamonera* is required to hold this ham in place (they only hang from roofs in bars and supermarkets), which is as typical on a Spanish kitchen counter as a blender is in the USA. A *jamonera* has a small O-shaped holder on top of a wooden arm that arches up from the base. This is where the hoof end goes. Once the hoof is through the hole, there is a screw to twist, which screws down and holds the leg firmly in place. On the base, there is a U-shaped holder. This is where the thigh end goes. The leg is in a diagonal position with the hoof up high. Cutting Spanish ham is an art. I have never even attempted, but recognize the excellence of a thin slice of perfect cured meat.

There is nothing more rewarding after a long, hot day of work than slicing open a yellow honeydew melon and wrapping slice of Spanish ham around a juice wedge. The sweet and salty combination is absolute perfection.

There are many types of *jamón serrano*. *Jamón serrano* is the general term and would be the lower end of the spectrum because, once the quality increases, it goes by more specific names like *Jamón Ibérico*, Iberian ham. Within this category are many others such as *pata negra*, black hoof, which refers to a certain type of pig that yields amazing ham. A good ham here is as important as a good wine, if not more so.

Whereas *jamón serrano* is something produced and consumed on a national level, *sobrassada* and *carnixulla* are produced in a more local atmosphere.

Sobrassada is one of those foods that it is better not to know what it is until after you eat it, which was luckily my case. I had fallen in love with it long before I knew it was raw, fermented sausage. I had seen it hanging from roofs (it seems that many meats unique to Spain hang from roofs) in old farmhouses. I have even seen storage rooms dedicated to this, with nails sticking out of the wooden beams to hold the *sobrassada* and the floor covered in old newspaper to catch the drippings.

I was first introduced to *sobrassada* at the restaurant *Es Molí de Foc*. They gave us a free small appetizer (typical in nice Menorcan restaurants that care about repeat customer and not only the hoards of tourists) of a slice of freshly toasted bread with something on it. I asked Fernando what it was and he said, "*Sobrassada*, very fattening, but very good." He took a bite and added, "With honey dribbled on top."

I asked him if he would show it to me in the supermarket and he said he would. A few days later, he made good on his promise. In the supermarket, there was a wooden stand with a wooden bottom (to catch the drippings) dedicated to just *sobrassada*. There were many different shapes, some thick, fat and vertical, while others were long and thin, with the ends tied together, making a kind of horseshoe shape. I chose one of these and I was just about to grab it when Fernando yelled out, "Stop!"

I stopped, surprised by his tone, and waited for an explanation.

"*Sobrassada* is extremely greasy, which is why there is always something catching its drippings. Grab a plastic bag and pick it up that way so you do not stain yourself."

Now I understood why the *sobrassada* wooden erection was right next to the vegetable section. I grabbed a plastic vegetable/fruit bag that was hanging next to the scale,[11] put

---

[11] The scale is not there just so you have an idea of how much you are buying. It is there because you have to weigh your own fruit and vegetables. You put your plastic bag full of whatever it is there, push the number that is beside the given fruit or vegetable and a ticket comes out with the weight and the price. You slap this on your bag and this is what they cover you at the counter. There is no one controlling this. I could easily go back after weighing and add a few more tomatoes and no one would ever know. However, I do not do this because this system

it on my hand reverse style like I have seen good citizens do when picking up their dog's crap off the sidewalk, and grabbed my *sobrassada.*

After my trip to the supermarket, I went to the bread store to get a fresh baguette of bread. I realized too late that I should have done this in reverse order, buying the heaviest items last. Later that night, I turned on the oven, sliced up the bread, put mozzarella on half of the bread slices (half of them with no cheese for Fernando), cut open the clear coating (I don't want to know what the clear coating is because I suspect it has something to do with pig's intestines) and pulled out the soft *sobrassada.* I placed chunks of it on the bread slices and popped it all in the oven. When the mozzarella had melted and the bread had toasted, I pulled them out and dribbled local honey over each piece. Juices had escaped from the *sobrassada* and soaked into the toasted bread. It was a huge success.

Carnixulla is also raw sausage, but it is cured instead of fermented. This *embutido* came to the island with the Romans and is still a popular dish over two thousand years later. This is my husband's favorite cold meat, which is perfect for me because, when I am too tired or too lazy to make dinner, I can always pacify him with a few slices of carnixulla. Its clear coating, which is whiter than the coating of *sobrassada* (though I suspected it as being the same element as with *sobrassada,* just whiter because of how it is processed), is easy to peel off once wetted with hot water. After peeling, which is not necessary, depending on the person's likes, it just needs to be sliced. This with a bit of bread and my husband is content.

*   *   *   *

is so indicative of the Menorcan relaxed attitude that I would never do anything to put it at risk.

The concept of first course or first plate and second course or second plate took me a long time to assimilate. The way I see it, it is just more dishes to wash. However, it turned out easier for me to accept more dish washing than for Fernando to run the risk of his salad touching his meat.

Spaniards have a very clear idea of what can be served as a first course and what can be served as a second course, which I did not grasp at first. I remember that one of Fernando's and my most vicious arguments took place after a long day of work for both of us. I asked Fernando what he wanted for dinner and he said something light because he was not too hungry. I looked in the fridge at what I could make and thought, *perfect; let's do soup and salad.*

I brought out the salad and we pleasantly chatted about the long day we had. All hell broke loose when I brought out the soup.

"Lana, soup is also a first course. We can't eat two first plates."

I looked at him with all the annoyance I felt and asked, "Why the hell not?"

"Because we just can't. It doesn't work."

"Let me get this straight; you cannot eat soup after salad because it doesn't work?"

"NO! I can't eat soup after salad because they are both first courses!"

There are times in a marriage when one would like to kill the other and this was definitely one of those times. I could easily see myself brutally killing Fernando and then sitting down to enjoy my nice bowl of soup that had followed my salad. Instead, I just started screaming about how stupid Europeans were, which prompted Fernando to start about how all Americans like to do is eat hamburgers and drop bombs on poor countries.

No one ate the soup and Fernando slept on the couch, both of us still thinking that we were right and that the other was a jackass.

12

A Bad Day Fixed

I have the most amazing handbag. I cannot call it a purse because it is not. To me, a purse implies frilliness or current fashion trends. My handbag is neither. If it must be stereotyped into a genre, then it is a classic in the making. Maybe handbag is not the correct word either, because I never hold it in my hand. It has a long strap that goes over my shoulder, crosses over my chest and back and rests its bulk on my hip and upper thigh. It is a deep, dark, rich leather… the kind that looks better with use. Menorca is known for amazing leather products and I was not let down. The fabric inside is the color of dried wheat just before harvest. It is the perfect size. I can carry large books and important papers without having to fold them. However, unlike many bags that offer the same, it is not horizontal, but vertical. Horizontal bags of this size look nice when full, but seem to double over on themselves when not. They also usually have a flap that I consider bothersome. However, my vertical bag is all zippers and pockets. It has the exact perfect amount of pockets. The zipper on the front is where I keep my cards… ID, credit, driver's license, etc. Above that is a little marsupial pouch where I drop things that I want fast access to like my cell phone, car keys, directions to where I am going and such.

The main part of the bag has a zipper with a wonderful leather pull. Past the main zipper is another pocket with a zipper, which is where I keep my 'on the run' makeup, tampons, comb and extra hair bands. Opposite this pocket are two long and narrow pouches; one is for pencils and one is for pens. The rest is for larger objects such as the current book I am reading, daily planner, notebook, stuff that needs to be mailed, and everything else. On the outside that lies against my leg is another zipper pocket. This pocket is ideal for boarding passes and passport. I only become OCD when I travel, which is often. I have to check at least two hundred times that I have my tickets and passport. I realize that every time that I check, I increase the risk of them being lost by falling out, or theft, but it is something that I must do[12]. This zipper pocket placed against my body reassures me enough that sometimes I can make an entire trip and only check ninety-nine times.

I bought this bag during my first year here in Menorca. I am not a bag-buying kind of person, but when I saw this bag in the window, I could feel the softness of the leather and the smell the deep, musk scent even before entering the

---

[12] I have to add the following because it reminds me of my OCD behavior, but am doing so as a footnote so readers can choose whether or not venture on this pointless digression. My friend, Christy, had understandable anxiety while in the last year of her Ph.D. Her anxiety took a strange form… Whenever she drove, especially at night, she became convinced that she had run someone over. She was so able to convince herself of this that she would often actually drive back along the road that she had just driven looking for run-over bodies. When she confided in me about this, I pointed out the fact that she was increasing her odds of running someone over every time she went back to check for bodies. When this did not get the laugh I had hoped for, I told her that if she actually ran a human being over, she would know without a doubt and would most likely have signs of such an accident on her vehicle. I now understand why my words of wisdom were of no help and why she continued to look for flattened bodies.

store. Its appearance was nice, but rustic. Quality and practically in one perfect object. I was discouraged when the lady in the store told me the price was 89€. I could buy a plane ticket to somewhere in Europe for that price. I walked out disillusioned and then came back five minutes later having convinced myself that, if I used the bag for life, it was worth it. After paying, I was asked if I wanted a bag for my purchase. I lifted the strap over my head and placed it on my shoulder. No bag for my bag required. Later that night, Fernando saw my new accessory (because I never have accessories, it was quite obvious) and asked me how much it had cost. At that moment, I started a tradition. I told him it cost exactly half of what it really cost.

I have had this bag for six years now. It has traveled to many parts of the world with me. It is the equivalent of my security blanket or teddy bear. When I am nervous, I stroke its soft, smooth leather. When I am terrified, I hug it on my lap as I do on all flights. I have even, when flying, turned down the much-coveted emergency exits with extra leg room because they require me to place my bag in the overhead compartment for takeoff and landing, which are exactly the critical moments in which I need to hug my bag. When I need an extra dose of relaxation, I place my nose against it and inhale its deep, rich sent.

I have been ridiculed for bringing my bag out dancing or to bars with clothing that does 'not go with it'. But I do not care... I feel uncomfortable and naked without it. I hope that I am never mugged because I am sure the mugger would not understand if I asked if I could give him the entire contents of the bag, but not the bag itself.

Once in Argentina, Fernando and I were enjoying dinner at a friend's house. We were well into the night and I was sick of my loose hair and was looking in the inner zipper pocket for a hair band. To my horror, I saw that the ripe wheat color fabric had torn and the contents of the pocket had escaped to the main part of the bag. My dear friend, Silvana, saw my expression, and asked me what was wrong. I told her that the inner pocket had torn. She took one more look at my face, then at the well-used leather, and ran upstairs. Silvana is one of those amazing people who can understand every kind of situation without having to have heard an explanation, and, best of all, she does not judge people for weird and irrational behavior. A few minutes later, she was walking down the stairs with a light brown spool of thread and needle. She glided her hands towards me as one does when offering to hold a newborn, and I handed over my baby. She stitched up the wound with amazing accuracy, especially considering the amount of red wine we had all ingested. When she was finished, she apologized that the thread was a darker shade than the wheat colored thread that matched the fabric. I hugged her and honestly told her that I was happy that what she had done for me was visible.

Another memorable moment is marked on my bag via wax. Fernando and I had just finished a lovely dinner of seafood and white wine after a hard day's work. It was a wonderful and balmy night, and we decided to go for a gin and tonic on a roof terrace (the name of the Menorcan bar and town will remain nameless because I would like to continue going there on occasion). I was pleasantly surprised that the only light on the terrace was candle light and the moon's reflection off the sea. We ordered our gin and tonics and enjoyed. While we were sipping, I commented on how the orange candle holder was the exact color of the chairs on our patio and of our summer bed cover. I also admired it for its simplicity; copper wire frame with orange glass that let the light of a tea candle slip through.

After a wonderfully relaxing time of enjoying the subtle roof terrace breeze, the moonlit sea view and a tasty beverage, Fernando asked for the bill. The gin and tonics were a bit overpriced, which was completely understandable considering the ambiance and view. However, in my buzzed state, I decided not to be understanding at the moment and used the overpriced drinks as a justifier for my stealing of the candle holder. When our change had been delivered, and the waiter turned and walked away, I quickly blew out the tea candle and slipped it into my bag. We walked out nonchalantly like the perfect customers we were not. When we arrived home twenty minutes later, I pulled out my trophy. As I did, I noticed that my hand brushed something hard that was not supposed to be hard. On closer inspection, I realized that the entire wax content of the tea candle (which is a surprisingly abundant amount considering the size) had coated the interior of my bag. I scraped the wax out as best I could. The remaining stain serves me as a perfect reminder that karma exists.

*   *   *   *

I was having a very bad day. I woke up to unbelievable heat and was already sticky with sweat at 7 am. I had been notified the previous night that my one day off per week was going to be interrupted because the girl who we hired as a receptionist had an urgent doctor's appointment. I was annoyed because I did not believe her, but lacked the *cojones* to demand a doctor's note for her absence.

As I showered, Fernando yelled at me for my lack of water conservation. Yes, I had showered the night before, but the heat was truly unbearable and I cannot accept sweating at 7 am. Of course, I did not tell Fernando any of this and let him criticize uninterrupted, which increased my annoyance of the day and furthered my lack-of-*cojones* feeling.

I opened the refrigerator door and remembered that I had drunk the last of the orange juice the previous morning and was planning on buying more on my *day off.* I slammed the refrigerator door shut and heard various things fall inside. I decided not to look and went to brush my teeth only to see in the mirror that I was having an ugly face day. I normally like my appearance, but I have certain days that I find my face atrocious. I have asked others on these days if they notice anything different about my face and they never seem to. However, I know when I am having an ugly face day, despite what my unobservant friends say. I tried to apply more makeup than usual, which ended up in me looking like a cheap street hooker. I tied my bun on top of my head instead of pulling it to the base of my skull like normal. I put on my favorite dress and shoes. I walked out of the bathroom feeling a bit better until I crossed Fernando in the hallway and heard his wonderful comment of, "Lana, you look a bit bloated today."

I replied in my head, *get fucked,* but just smiled at him like I was not hurt by his objective observation. I decided that I was going to be *bored* that night in bed so that he also felt insecure. I made a pact with myself that if he made another ungracious remark (forget the fact that it may be honest) during my ugly face day, I would even fake a yawn during.

I got into my car and started off to work. I was halfway there when a suicidal finch flew in front of my car. I had no time to react and hit the finch full on. I felt terrible, but honestly knew there was no way I could have avoided the collision. I stopped my car and saw its little body twitching on the road. I walked back to where it was and realized that its back must be broken. No hope for this little guy. I did not want it to suffer with a broken back, lying on the hot road until it finally died, so I picked it up and wrang its neck. Anyone who has grown up on a farm knows that this is a very efficient and relatively painless way to kill a bird. However, the car that came around the corner while I was standing in the middle of the road with the little bird's head in my fist, swirling its body around in quick circular motions, was occupied by people who were obviously not from a farm. They slowed, almost to a stop, with their mouths agape. I saw their eyes travel from the dead bird, to me, then to my car, which unfortunately was the work van, and I thought, *oh shit,* as they read, 'Ecomuseo de Cap de Cavalleria'. This did not look like a very eco-friendly act. They looked from the van to me, back to the van and then back to me. I just shrugged, dead bird dangling from my hand.

I finally arrived at the museum and opened up praying that the non-farm tourist would not pay a visit.

They did not. The only thing that visited me was the horrendous heat. I made myself an espresso only to find that I was unable to drink it because of the extreme heat. My body just said, 'no'.

Five hours later, the receptionist showed up after her *urgent* doctor's appointment. I do not recall ever having looked so cheerful after an urgent doctor's appointment, but decided to let it pass because I had spent all of my energy on sweating and killing birds. I grabbed my wonderful bag brusquely in some sort of attempt to convey my disbelief and annoyance of this new worker only to have my bag fall to the floor. This kind of shit always happens to me. For example, I no longer slam doors to depict my anger because half of the time I slam my finger in the slamming door, which kind of ruins the emotion that I was trying to express. I felt like this as I bent down to pick my bag up off the floor. The strap had busted out of the seam. The receptionist, in her bubbly state, offered to tell me about a shoe maker in her town who could most likely fix my bag. "He lives right next to me and works out of his garage. When the garage door is open, that means he is receiving customers. If it is closed, that means that he is not."

I proceeded to the street that the evil new worker had given me and saw four identical green garage doors, all closed. I walked to the corner to an internet café and asked if he knew were the shoemaker lived. "His is the first garage door, but he is eighty-five years old, and only fixes things when he wants to. If his garage door is not open, don't wait around."

Perfect.

I decided I would swing by the nearest town, Ferreries. There was a fabric store there and the woman who owned it mended clothes. I doubted that she would be able to fix such thick leather, but thought it was worth a try. I was sweaty, uncomfortable and irritable when I walked into the fabric store. I was greeted by name by the woman at the counter. I was surprised because we had only met once a year ago when I brought a dress with a busted seam. I felt a little better and asked if she could help me and showed her my injured bag. "Not a chance; you need to visit a shoemaker." She told me that there was a shoemaker, *zapatero*, in Ferreries, but he was a *character*.

Shit, I thought to myself. When Menorcan people say *character*, it is a euphemism for asshole or crazy person.

She proceeded to explain, "If he is having a good day, he will fix what you need. But if he is having a bad day, he will tell you it is impossible to fix and ask you to leave."

Wonderful. Just what I needed on this crappy day; a *character* who fit both meanings of the euphemism.

"But maybe Xavi can help you."

I looked at her enthusiastically, waiting for more Xavi information.

"Xavi is a *tapicero*."

I was not really sure what that was, but assumed if he could help me that it must have something to do with upholstery or leather.

"His shop is two streets down."

"Does it say *tapicero* on the building?"

"No, no. He works out of his garage. It has a green door."

Fantastic... another green door. That was extremely helpful information being that all shutters and garage doors are painted green in Menorca.

She must have seen the doubt in my face because she added, "Just walk two streets down and ask for Xavi."

"Do I just knock on his green garage door or is there a doorbell?"

"No, no... Just open the door and go in. That is what everyone does at Xavi's."

I was considering anew the shoemaker *character*, but was concerned that it may also be another green garage door, so I decided to try for Xavi first. I walked down to the second street and saw rows of green garage doors. Luckily, there was an old lady sitting on the sidewalk in a fold-out chair fanning herself. I asked her if she knew where Xavi, the *tapicero*, had his shop.

To my enormous relief, she said, "That is Xavi right there in the green shirt."

He was talking to someone who had stopped their car in the middle of the road for a chat. When he finished, I asked if he was Xavi. He nodded affirmative and I told him that the lady in the fabric store had said that maybe he could help me. I held out my bag for his inspection. He clapped me on the back and said, "I sure can, come on."

He opened the green garage doors and my suspicions were confirmed – he was an upholsterer. I thought that we were going to stop at the front where the desk was so that I could take the contents of my bag out and set a time to come back for it, but he waved me to the back of the shop and plunked down at a sewing machine. While he looked for the perfect color of thread, I took the larger things out of my bag. He found the thread that he had been looking for, placed it where it needed to go in the machine and motioned for my bag. I was surprised at how gently he was able to sew through two thick layers of leather.

When he was confident with his job, he took my bag in two hands and pulled the newly sewn strap as hard as he could from the bag. I almost cried out because he looked very strong and could probably tear metal, and surely leather. However, the bag did not break and the new stitching did not budge. He stood up, handed me my bag, clapped me on the back again and, as he turned to walk away, said, "There you go."

As I shoved things back into my back, I called out, "How much do I owe you?"

He turned and smiled the smile that only truly good people can, the kind that feels like a sun's ray touching your frozen nose on a cold day, and said, "I am not going to charge you for that. That was nothing. Take care."

Then off he went out the green garage doors. As I left the garage, I hugged my bag and thought, *what another nice memory with my lovely bag.*

Xavi had not only fixed my bag, but also my day.

13

A Log with Bowel Movements

Living on Menorca is very much like a happy and healthy marriage; no matter how great it is, a little break or get away is necessary for one's sanity and continuance. The mainland is usually the destination for this wee-break and, with one of the most beautiful and culturally rich cities in the world only being thirty minutes away, Barcelona is usually the place to go for this little get away.

Flying is my choice mode of transportation, especially because I receive a forty percent discount on flights to and from the Balearic Islands because of my residency here[13].

---

[13] At least up until recently. The discount now only applies to people born with in the European community. Most people feel that this is a subtle form of discrimination, assuming directed at South and Central Americans and people from Africa, who are coming in greater numbers each year to work on the islands. It has been a topic of much debate and most people (even those not affected) think it is unfair. The discount was created because the airfare to and from the islands is inflated due to tourism. Therefore, they created the discount for people who live on the islands. But now it is only if you are a born European

However, this is not an option when one wants to take one's car.

The tourist season was finally over and so was our work both in the museum and the archaeological excavations. Fernando and I were both teetering on the edge of sanity and decided that Barcelona and surrounding areas would be a perfect place to spend Christmas, forgoing friends and family (as to not put our sanity in further jeopardy). Because we wanted to explore Catalonia, we decided to take our car, which means the ferry. There is a new, fast ferry that only takes four hours, but it is twice as expensive as the ferry that takes nine hours. Working for a non-profit organization = nine-hour ferry, which unfortunately is usually more expensive per person than the thirty-minute flight, not counting the cost of the car.

We boarded the ferry around 9 pm, stowed the car and went to claim our place in the lounge before everyone else realized that that was the best place to sleep (for the cheap people like us who do not pay for a cabin) because you could stretch out on the sofas as opposed to sitting in the airplane like seats. We ordered two gin and tonics to justify our presence on the sofa and placed belongings on either side of us so that, once people did get the idea to come and sleep there, we had our territory marked.

After a night of extreme discomfort, despite the fact that we had the best place on the ship, we awoke to a vacuum cleaner in our ears. The sun had yet to rise, but we were almost in Barcelona and they were getting the ship

---

and live on the island. A non-European can live and work on the island for forty years and still not receive the discount. However, a European can come to the island to work for the summer, change their current address to one here (for their short stay) and receive the discount.

ready for the return trip. On the sofa next to us, a Catalan man complained about how rude it was of them to be cleaning the bar while we were sleeping.

The guy with the vacuum cleaner said, "Technically, when I closed the bar last night at two, I should have thrown you all out, but I did not because I felt bad because you were all sleeping. But don't worry; from now on, I will throw everyone out of the lounge at 2 am on the dot so as to not wake up anyone with the vacuum cleaner at 6 am."

Everyone who had slept in the lounge shot the guy a 'thanks asshole' look and we all began to gather our belongings. I completely sympathized with the barman... Nothing is more annoying than doing a favor only to have it backfire.

Hoping that I would not be forced into standard seating on the way back, I said to the barman as we walked out of the lounge, "Thank you for letting us sleep in the lounge. I hope that one jerk does not ruin it for all of us."

His reply was a grunt that implied 'I'll think about it'.

We descended to where we had left our car and got in. We left the ferry and port area and were thrust into the center of Barcelona. Thank God it was only 6 am and the traffic was not too dense because we were overwhelmed as it was. Luckily, Fernando was driving. On Menorca, I am used to two-lane roads, caution signs with cows on them, cattle guards, etc. The four-lane, one-way roundabout with stoplights throughout it on exiting the port was more than I could handle. It is hard to even *find* a stoplight in Menorca. Fortunately, Fernando, having studied and lived in Barcelona for nine years, knew what to do while I sat beside him in awe. Nine months on the island proved to be too much for integration into the real world.

We drove to the outskirts of Barcelona to a small town in the mountains called Vallromanes, where we have a tiny studio. We unpacked our belongings and took a long nap, recovering the sleep that we had missed the previous night. When evening time rolled around, we decided to go visit the city. Fernando had told me that there is a huge Christmas market in front of the cathedral, and I was eager to see it and feel festive.

Fernando had explained to me when I asked about his childhood Christmases that Bethlehem scenes are the central Christmas decoration in each house. Also, each town has their own public Bethlehem scene on a large scale. They are important all throughout Spain because they are what most do instead of a Christmas tree, which I found very environmentally friendly and, indeed, very practical because there are hardly any trees left in Spain. It also struck me as a bit more sensible to celebrate the birth of Jesus Christ with a scene portraying and honoring his birth instead of the Pagan tradition of decorating trees.

I realized when we entered the Christmas market that, just like we have special Christmas tree ornaments, people here have special Bethlehem figurines, some passed down through the family, new additions each year and figurines that are unique to certain places, which reminded me of our cowboy paraphernalia Christmas tree ornaments in Red Bluff.

As we walked among the different stalls selling Bethlehem figurines, one kept jumping out as *different*... It was a guy with a red hat taking a dump. Some had little piles of shit below the guy defecating while others showed him in mid stride. But there was no doubt about it... it was a figurine of a guy crapping. At first, I thought that it was just a weird stall that included this rude figurine. When I realized that every stall carried this surprising Bethlehem character, I asked Fernando about it. He laughed, realizing for the first time that it was a bit strange if you were not accustomed to seeing it, and explained that the figurine was typical in Catalan Bethlehem scenes and the name of this character was *Caganer*. This is the Catalan addition to the Bethlehem scene... baby Jesus, the three wise men, Mary, Joseph, and *Caganer* taking a dump in the corner or hidden behind the wall. The traditional *Caganer* wears a red sack-like hat called a *barretina* while he does his business.

We continued to stroll among the stalls and Fernando pointed out that there were variations to the traditional *Caganer*. On a shelf, I saw a pope *Caganer*, famous soccer player *Caganers*, famous actor *Caganers*, etc. I asked Fernando, "Do you think that they have an Obama *Caganer*?"

Before he could answer, the guy running the stall replied, "They are all sold out... everywhere. Everyone wanted an Obama *Caganer* this Christmas. But I still have Bush if you want."

I thanked the man, but declined the shitting Bush figurine.

I reflected back to the previous year and my Christmas with Fernando and friends on Menorca, but could recall no shitting Christmas traditions. However, I did notice that the Bethlehem scenes had their own local flavor. In Menorca, there are *Taula* figurines that are placed as the sacred area in the Bethlehem scenes. *Taulas* are the amazing standing stones that form a T-shape built by the *Talayotic* culture on Menorca. The *Taulas* are always found in the center of the *Talayotic* villages and most agree that this was their sacred area. And now these T-shape standing stones can be bought in miniature for Menorcan Bethlehems.

I mentioned to Fernando what I was thinking as we left the large market in front of the cathedral and passed through the Roman entrance of the city, making our way into the *Barrio Gótico*. "Menorca is so near to Barcelona, but I don't remember seeing even one shitting figurine."

Fernando laughed. "It is a Catalan thing only. But there is more than one shitting tradition in Catalonia." He laughed even harder when he saw my face. He continued, "I cannot imagine the holidays without a *Caga Tío*."

He explained that Catalan families get a log, paint a face on it, and prop the face end up with two sticks for legs. They then cover the back end with a blanket. This happy faced log is called *Caga Tío* or Uncle Shitter (that is about as close of a translation that I can come up with). Children will put the equivalent of milk and cookies out at night in front of him to drink and eat, fattening him up, filling his splintery intestines. On the night of the 24th, children hit the log with sticks chanting a song about *Caga Tío, Caga Tío,* encouraging him to *cagar* while parents reach up the blanket and pull out chocolate goodies and sweets for the kids that *Caga Tío* has supposedly shat out. I believe there can be variations in *Caga Tío's* bowel movements because I was later told by a five-year-old that last year *Caga Tío* had shat out new panties for her.

I asked Fernando if this was tradition that only some people participate in, not believing that the entire Catalan culture viewed this as normal. But no, he assured me that this is as true a Catalan tradition as putting up stockings on the 24th is for people in the USA. "You can even buy pre-made *Caga Tío* logs with their faces pre-painted and front stick-legs already in place, but I imagine you have to provide your own blanket in these cases."

We continued walking through the *Barrio Gotico* and Fernando pointed out a boutique that had pre-made *Caga Tíos* in the window. They, too, like the *Caganers*, were wearing little red *barretinas*. They looked so cute, I wanted to pet them. I could not imagine hitting their smiling little face with a stick, demanding bowel movements. I guess one must be Catalan to truly understand because Fernando, being Catalan, had no problem whatsoever and thought it was more strange that I thought all this shitting at

Christmas time strange, than him considering his cultural traditions strange.

I had Fernando take pictures of me next to the *Caga Tios* in the window while Catalan couples walked passed looking at me as if *I* was weird.

So, is this what people mean when they talk about being culturally enlightened?

And to think, Spain does not want to give Catalonia independence.

14

El Payés

The title *payés* was at first difficult for me to understand. I first understood it to be farmer. I am from a farming family and what the *payés* and his wife do is what my Aunt Anne and Uncle John do, and they are farmers. However, when I used the Spanish word *campesino* for farmer, I was told by Fernando never to use this term with the *payés* because he would be offended.

"Well, what would be the Spanish equivalent then?" I asked Fernando, a little annoyed that my Catalan-peppered Spanish was once again flawed.

"*Agricultor*," Fernando said slowly in case it was a new word for me, which it was, but it sounded enough like agriculture that it was easy to remember.

I thought to myself about the word and was sure it meant 'a person who works in agriculture'. It sounded like a farmer to me.

When I arrived home later that night, I typed *agricultor* into my Spanish-English dictionary and *farmer* popped out as the translation. I showed Fernando my results and he started to laugh.

"I love it... This is a situation where we Spaniards are more politically correct than you Yankees. I now understand what you mean. Ha ha ha. You get mad when I call a flight attendant a stewardess because it is not what they wish to be called anymore. What is it that you always say? 'There are many ways to call people what they are and everyone likes to be called what they personally want to be called and not the stereotypical name'," Fernando mocked me. "*Campesino* vs *payés* or *agricultor*, in Spanish, is a situation that deals with political correctness."

I could see Fernando was getting into professor mode and prepared myself for a lecture.

"Not too long ago in Spain, the majority of people dedicated their lives to working the land, even though the majority of them did not actually own land. With the majority of people working the land, the term *campesino* was quite general indeed. People wanted to feel unique, to distinguish themselves. A term that described a dirt-poor family taking care of a small patch of land could not be used for a person in charge of acres and acres of land. *Campesino* implies poor farmer and is even synonymous with peasant. *Agricultor* is someone who works large extensions of land. *Payés* is the term for *agricultor* in Catalonia and the Balearic Islands. Nowadays, the word *campesino* has so many negative connotations that it is best not to use anymore. You will never offend anyone by calling them an *agricultor* or *payés*. The *payés* here is in charge of the entire farm of Cavalleria and Santa Teresa. Before, there was a *payés* in charge of just Santa Teresa, but when he retired, the *payés* of Cavalleria absorbed Santa Teresa into his work load. Half of what he makes goes to Señor Olivar and he keeps the other half."

"What!" I exclaimed.

Fernando delighted in my shock, chuckled and continued, "Yep, half goes to Señor Olivar for the privilege of letting the *payés* and his family live there and work the land. Reminds you of the times of peasants and nobles, no? The *payés'* family has been working Señor Olivar's land for generations and I believe the arrangement has not changed through the centuries. There is a mutual respect between the families and it would be almost impossible for Señor Olivar to throw the *payés* off the land if he wanted to, because the agreement is now considered a tradition. It has more to do with honor than a contract."

"I wish our place was as secure here," I commented to Fernando. I always have a nagging fear that our contract will not be renewed when the time comes to sign again.

"Yeah, I would like the same security, but not at paying half of what we make. I had a hell of a time convincing Señor Olivar that I wanted to pay a straight forward annual rent. He had never heard of such a crazy idea."

After listening to Fernando's lecture, I now understood why I should call the farmer of Cavalleria *agricultor*, or even better, *el payés* in Catalan. This knowledge came at just the right time because, a few months later, a combination of using the correct title, showing my respect, and being covered in cow shit cooled a very heated situation.

* * * *

Like in many parts of the world, less and less Menorcans are dedicating their lives to agriculture. It is a hard way of making a living. There is an expression in Spain, '*Trabajando de sol a sol*' – working from sun to sun. To make a living off the land in Menorca, it is work from sun up until sun down and sometimes more. The fields are full of stones, the soil is not extremely fertile and water is scarce. Not the best farming conditions.

The *payés* of Cavalleria is not the easiest man to get along with, but he works harder than anyone I know; that alone gaining him the respect of others, especially of Señor Olivar, who reaps half of what the *payés* makes. The *payés* and Fernando are not the best of friends because their work seems to be often mutually exclusive.

For a week, Fernando and I noticed that the *payés* was repairing an ancient bridge that arched over a spring and marshy area that ran off into the port.

"Why in the world is he repairing that bridge?" I wondered out loud, curious because the *payés* is not a man to waste time on silly tasks.

"Maybe they are going to repair the small cottage up on the hill," Fernando speculated.

We both though it unlikely considering the amount of money that would need to be invested, but it seemed to be the only answer.

We promptly forgot about it and life continued on as normal until I caught a movement out of the corner of my eye while clearing one of the tables on the museum's terrace. I squinted towards the evening sun and could not believe what I saw... A huge yellow tractor in the Roman Necropolis. I now understood the bridge. The farmer had gone behind the tumbled-down cottage, cut a road through the forest, made a passage through a stone wall and was going to till the land now that Santa Teresa was his responsibility, since the *payés* of Santa Teresa retired the year before.

"Fernando! Fernando!" I screamed as I raced up the steps of the museum to the lab where Fernando was classifying Roman pottery. "There's a tractor in the Necropolis!"

Fernando visibly paled, raced to the window and bellowed out, "*Ostia puta!*"

As Fernando flew down the stairs, I yelled after him, "If it is the *payés*, be nice; he probably does not know that the area is a protected archaeological site."

"*Mi culo*," Fernando growled back before slamming the door and sprinting across the field.

Normally, I would have laughed. When I first tried saying 'my ass' in Spanish to convey my disbelief in something, Fernando told me there was no such saying in Spanish and that it sounded ridiculous. I continued to use it anyway and now Fernando cannot get through even one day without referring to his ass when doubtful. However, I was not in the mood to laugh because I know that Fernando is the least tactful person in existence when he is nervous and I easily imagined how the conversation was going to go.

Unfortunately, I was right on the mark with my imagined conversation between Fernando and the *payés*. It went something like this:

"What the hell do you think you are doing? This is a protected archaeological site; you cannot till this land. You cannot work this land."

"Who the hell are you to tell me what I can and cannot do? My family has been working this land for generations. I'll till wherever I want to. Get out of my way."

"You absolutely cannot till this land! If you continue, I will call the police and the heritage department and turn you in for the mass destruction of a protected archaeological site."

"You do just that. I'm going to have you thrown out of here before you make all of Cavalleria a declared archaeological site. The more you excavate, the more you find. And the more you find means the less I have to work with."

"You have tons of acres to till; why do you care about these ones? Can't you go and till elsewhere on the property? I am sure that there are more fertile areas than this wind-beaten, salt-burnt land."

"Don't tell me how to do my job."

"Fine, I won't, but I am telling you not to till this area."

"I'll do whatever I want."

When Fernando reiterated the conversation for me, I almost strangled him. Why are men so pigheaded? Fernando could only see his side and the *payés* his. I thought they both had very valid sides. Fernando wanted more than anything to protect and study the cultural heritage of the area. *El payés* wanted to continue working as he and his family had done for generations. I am sure he was not happy that he had spent so much energy in repairing the bridge to access the area only to have a crazy archaeologist running in front of his tractor.

The *payés* did stop after Fernando walked away, but I am sure he was not happy about it.

*   *   *   *

Until 2007, our archaeological project focused on the Roman military fort next to Santa Teresa. It was only a two-minute walk from the laboratory, where all of the excavated material goes for study, and was very convenient. However, the fort was almost completely excavated and Fernando felt it was a good time to start on the other side of the port where the Roman city of Sanisera was located.

We started figuring out the logistics of the project. We would divide it into two separate projects, the Roman City Dig and the Necropolis Dig. The city dig would focus on archaeology in general, classification of pottery and the urban structures of the city, while the necropolis dig would focus on the tombs on the outskirts of the city and would be geared toward those studying physical anthropology.

With that settled, we had one more issue to figure out; how were the students going to bring back the archaeological material and tools each day?

"We could use the bridge and the back road," Fernando suggested.

"You mean the one the *payés* fixed to till the land that you told him he could not work because of the archaeological site? He would rather blow it up than let you use it after that. Maybe if you offered to pay for the repairs and labor of the bridge... but I don't even think that would soften him."

Fernando agreed with me and we set out through the waist-high weeds to try to find an area that we could make into a road.

"Can't the students just walk back with the archaeological material and expensive tools every day, leaving the large, inexpensive tools on site? This is Menorca; no one is going to steal them. There is already a trail... It is only a fifteen-minute walk."

"No, no... We *must* have a road."

I had a feeling that this had to do more with Fernando's pigheadedness than anything else, and decided not to waste my energy being rational and logical. We continued on through the weeds, and decided that the only place to make a road to get to the site would be via knocking a hole through three stone walls.

Fernando showed his idea to Señor Olivar. He approved of the plan as long as the stones from the wall were dealt with neatly and that the holes in the walls would have the edges nicely finished so that they looked like passageways and not holes in the wall. We received permission from the city hall to create the dirt road that connected to the public road. They checked and double checked the small ancient bridge that we would be passing over. Fernando promised that only a small Renault 4 would pass over it carrying the tools and archaeological materials of the day. They agreed on that condition. Fernando called and reserved the services of Jose and tractor, who would make the road, knock the holes in the walls, and neatly carry away the rocks.

When Fernando hung up after making the tractor reservation, I asked, "How is the tractor going to get over the spring? The small bridge will not support its weight, which is why you promised we would only use the Renault 4 to cross it."

Fernando looked extremely sheepish and said, "I am going to use the *payés'* new bridge for just a few seconds."

"No you are not! He will kill you! Then I will re-kill you for getting killed!"

"I have permission from the owners of the land. I doubt he will even know. I will only be using it for a second. There is no lock on the gate, and I have permission from the owners," Fernando said, trying to convince us both.

We fought and fought, but I saw that I was not going to change his stubborn mind. The tractor arrived, used the bridge for a few seconds, and then was over the hill and out of sight. I sighed a huge sigh of relief when I could no longer see the yellow of its cab.

Jose and his tractor worked most of the day, following the instructions Fernando had given him in the morning. It was evening time when the phone rang in the museum. It was one of the students calling about another student.

"Lana, Lacey cut her leg open on the rocks near the beach. She is definitely going to need stitches. She is pretty upset. Could you please come and take her to the hospital?"

I wracked my brain and tried and tried to remember which one was Lacey, and yelled '*mierda*' when I remembered who she was. Of course, she was the one underage student we had accepted that year and she had a note saying that Fernando Contreras was responsible for her while here. *Shit; shit; shit.* Why do students always hurt themselves on their day off? I called Fernando and could not believe my luck that he was in one of the very few points with cell phone coverage in the Roman city. I heard the tractor working away in the background while I explained the situation. It looked like Fernando and I both had to go; he to sign any necessary hospital paperwork, being her temporary guardian, and me to calm her down and translate for Fernando.

I ran through the closing procedures with the staff and they assured me they could close without me. By the time I had finished with my interrogation of the staff on closing, Fernando had arrived panting from the hike from the Roman city and was ready to go. We set off towards Ciutadella and the injured student.

"Jose is still working with his tractor, but said he would be done within the hour. Let's deal with the student, eat somewhere in Ciutadella and go home."

The plan sounded great to me, even though I was worried about a confrontation between the *payés* and the unsuspecting Jose.

Lacey needed fourteen stitches and handled it very well. I can only imagine how scary it must have been for a seventeen-year-old girl to be sewn up in a foreign country. Once she was fixed, we delivered her safe and sound to the student residence.

Fernando paid for dinner at a nice restaurant in Ciutadella, trying his hardest to be upbeat and pleasant, knowing that I was not pleased with the tractor situation. I decided to forgive him, and enjoyed my evening of wining and dining.

I woke up to Fernando's ritual kiss goodbye, contemplated my hangover from the wining and dining, and went back to sleep hoping that my throbbing head would not be throbbing when I re-awoke in an hour and a half to go to work.

It was still throbbing. I had a horrible hangover face and tried to compensate with nice clothes. I put on a new pair of amazingly stretchy jeans that my mom had recently sent me, understanding that special pants were needed in order to fit over my very voluptuous ass and not be ridiculously large in the waist. I slipped on a pair of open-toed, cork-bottomed clogs that boosted me up a few inches, making me feel tall and sexy. I put on a fitted, sky blue tank-top and decided to top it off with my new white linen shirt, which I left unbuttoned and rolled the sleeves up to my elbows. I pondered over my reflection for a few minutes and decided that I looked casually chic and felt much better about going to work with a hangover.

Pre-caffeine Lana, even with chic, casual clothing, was still not up to going to work, and I decided for a tar-thick espresso. Post-caffeine Lana was much more prepared to face the day, and I stared the journey to work after stalling my ancient Renault 4 three times. I managed to pass the milk-gathering truck without incident and was beginning to feel a bit better until I saw yellow in the distance. "Shit," I screamed to the steering wheel.

The yellow was the cab of the Jose's tractor and, if I was calculating the distance correctly, it was right next to the *payés'* bridge.

"Shit. Shit. Shit. Shit," I yelled at my steering wheel.

Jose had left his tractor overnight when working for us before, but always left it in the museum parking. He surely thought that it would be better to leave it protected behind a fence, having no idea that we did not want the *payés* to see it.

When I rounded the corner, my 'shits' became 'fucks'. It appeared that the *payés* had been up long before me and had been busy. There was huge metal and wood cart blocking the gate directly in front of the new bridge, which was the only way the tractor could leave the field.

I don't remember how, but my car managed to find its way and park in the museum's parking while my ears rang and my heart thudded at an unsafe rhythm. As I got out of my car, I heard my name pronounced in an unpleasant tone.

I turned and noticed for the first time that I was not alone in the parking. Jose was also there and wanted to know what was going on. He had not finished the road, had been planning on doing so before noon, but was now unsure because there was obviously a problem and he did not want to become involved.

I completely understood his feelings; I did not want to be involved either. I thought to myself, *if I kill Fernando, will the problem be fixed?* I rejected the idea because, even though it might help the current situation, Fernando's death via my hand would bring with it its own problems.

I told Jose to hold tight and ran down to the Roman military fort where Fernando was excavating with students. "Did you happen to notice the wee little problem we have?"

"Yes," Fernando admitted unhappily.

"Jose is here and wants to know what is going on with his tractor that appears to be imprisoned."

"*Mierda.* I had no idea he was going to leave it there. I thought he was going to finish up last night."

"Fernando, don't try to pass the blame."

He hung his head and followed me up the trail to where Jose was waiting.

After talking a bit with Fernando, Jose decided to have a chat with the *payés*. After an hour, Jose came back and told us that the *payés* apologized for the inconvenience to Jose; however, he was not moving the cart. Needless to say, he was not happy that Fernando had used his bridge without his permission, especially because it was Fernando who had rendered the bridge useless.

Jose was in distress. He had a full work load for the rest of the day, week and month. He could not afford to miss a day because his tractor was being held captive due to a standoff between two very stubborn men.

Fernando offered to pay Jose's fee for as long as the tractor was trapped, which was about 500€ per day. Jose was not happy about the situation, but realized there was no immediate solution. Fernando told him that he would keep him posted and Jose walked off mumbling.

Fernando decided that he was going to go have a chat with the *payés*. He was back in less than ten minutes.

"So what happened?" I eagerly asked while knives sliced at my intestines.

"He told me to get off his property or he would call the police."

"Shit. What are you going to do?"

"I am going to call the police myself."

"Shit… that is not going to help matters, Fernando."

His answer was to pick up the phone and call the police, explaining that he had permission from the owner to be on the land, but that his hired tractor was being held captive by the *payés*.

I tried to get through the day as normal, but my nervous diarrhea continually interrupted my attempts at normalcy. Around 6:30 pm, the police showed up. They had talked to the *payés* and explained to Fernando that there was nothing they could do. They, being two locals, explained to Fernando that a *payés* and a land owner are like associates... partners. Because we passed through a part of the owner's land that was worked on by the *payés* and not by us, we also had to have had his permission. The *payés* was within his rights to lock the gate of the land that he worked, even if it was via a huge wood and metal cart.

This was obviously *not* what Fernando wanted to hear. He looked like he was going to collapse with stress, when I decided that I was going to go and talk with the *payés*.

"No, you are not!" Fernando shouted.

"Yes, I am!" I shouted back. "We would not be in this situation if you had listened to me in the first place. There is no one left to talk with the *payés* except me. He knows I represent you… but I do so in a way that does not piss him off as much as you do."

It was now around 8 pm and the sun was about to set. I drove the five minutes to the *payés'* ranch, drove up his long dirt driveway and parked by his house. I walked up to the house, but no one seemed to be there except for a hysterical black dog that repeatedly jumped up on me, staining my white linen shirt with dark red dirt. I decided to smile at the dog instead of doing other things to it that came to mind in case someone was watching out of the window. I walked around the house towards the barn and found the eldest of the *payés'* boys putting away various tools that had been used during the day.

"*El Payés?*" I asked.

"Milking the cows."

I followed his extended finger to the long, barn-like structure a few hundred meters in the distance. I hiked my way over there and had to shove my way through the cows that were forming two lines, one on each side of the building. There were three entrances to the building. The cows were using the two on the extremes, so I opted for the one in the center. I was a bit unsure, as large cows mooed on either side of me, but then I heard a 'yup, yup' noise coming from inside, which sounded somewhat human, so I ventured a bit further, down two of the four steps of the center entrance.

"*Señor payés?*" I said, realizing for the first time that I did not know his actual name. "Can I speak with you?"

"I am working. If you want to talk to me, you have to come in here and talk while I work."

The center entrance was lower by about a meter than the two side entrances where the cows were entering. They walked along the two waist-high lanes, while the farmer applied cream to their udders, then a metal device that looked like an udder with hoses connected to each of the nipple-shaped apparatuses. When he pulled the metal-udder milking device off the cow's udder, he yelled 'yup, yup' and the cow proceeded to leave the building out of the opposite side to where I assumed they would be fed.

As I gingerly walked down the two remaining steps, I took in the *payés'* milking attire: rubber boots, rubber apron, and an old, crusty looking hat. The meaning of his clothes hit me at the exact same moment that a shit-covered cow tail smacked me across the face. Seconds later, another cow in the milking line managed to project her shit onto my shoulder. The *payés* looked amused and then tried to hide it, remembering that he was angry with us. Surprise was next to register on his face when he saw that the cow shit did not faze me. He couldn't know that I was champion of cow-pie Frisbee on my ranch back home. I shoved my corked-bottom, open-toed shoes ankle deep into the carpet of cow feces and waded over to where the *payés* was standing.

I apologized profusely for Fernando's lack of respect. Of course he should have asked permission first.

I tried my first tactic. "Do you know the archaeological boundaries of the Roman city of Sanisera were not set by Fernando? They were set by a random archaeologist who the heritage department hired. Fernando says that they are too large and, as he studies the area, he can reduce the limits so that you can work part of that land that was previously unworkable. Furthermore, the dirt that we take out of the excavation can go onto your land, making it more workable."

"I don't care. I don't want anyone on the land. I want it to be the way it was when I was a boy; no tourists and no archaeologists! What do I care about a measly parcel of land with extra dirt?"

It was too bad that the *payés* and Fernando disliked each other so much, because they were similar in so many ways: serious, hardworking, uncompromisingly stubborn...

"*Señor payés*, I understand your sentiments; however, that is impossible now even if we were no longer here. Can't we just compromise and find a solution that makes everyone happy?"

"The problem is, when Fernando wants to do something, you find out about it afterwards," the *payés* observed.

What could I say to that? It was the perfect truth. Fernando's life motto seems to be 'it is easier to ask for forgiveness than for permission'. I knew this way better than the *payés*. Too bad Fernando wanted to be cremated and have his ashes sprinkled out to sea because I would have loved to have (at that uncomfortable, cow-shit-covered moment) written this frigging motto on his tombstone. But, all I could do was nod my head and promise (tactic number two) that I would keep Fernando under control, that the archaeology students would walk and that no one would use the bridge.

"I promise that we won't use the bridge if you remove the cart. Only Jose will go in, get his tractor, and leave directly."

The *payés* milked his cows in silence for the next few minutes while the cows continued to splatter me with dung. When he turned to give me his answer, I could again see that he was trying to hide his amusement at my shit-splattered state.

"I'll think about it. Tonight I am going to finish up here, shower, eat and go to bed. Maybe tomorrow; I don't know. I'll think about it."

I happily told him that was more than enough and that I was grateful for him considering it. I said goodbye and walked back to my car.

The powers of the universe continued to favor me and I found a plastic bag in the trunk to sit on so as to not stain the car seats with cow dung. On the drive back home, I realized that our entire conversation had been in Spanish. He could have easily used my not speaking Menorquín against me. I had experienced angry Catalan tourists in the museum and almost all used my lack of Catalan against me. 'Your dog needs to be put on a leash while in the patio', or 'excuse me, the tables are for customers only' many times elicits the reply, 'don't tell me what to do unless you can tell me in Catalan'.

However, I have never found this to be the case in Menorca. Every Menorcan who I have met happily switches from Menorquín to Spanish if it helps the conversation without calling attention to what they are doing. On the other hand, many Catalan people refuse to switch or make you very aware that they are doing so with great annoyance. I often feel that Catalan is as much a social (and political) weapon as a language, whereas I have never felt this with Menorquín.

I thought again about the *payés* and smiled. A perfect example of Menorcan manners. He was extremely within his rights to be angry with me (as I was representing Fernando and archaeologists), yet he never resorted to the easiest way of not speaking with me and making me feel bad. Menorcans are well known for their kindness and hospitality. I can see why. The *payés*, even though he felt disrespected and angry, switched to a language that was more difficult and less familiar for him so that the conversation would be easier for me. And I did not even know he had done so until I reflected on the drive home.

Before I went to sleep, I told Fernando for the millionth time that he was an ass and should have listened to me in the first place.

The next morning, I saw the yellow of the tractor in the same place that I had the day before. I rounded the corner and almost crashed into the stone wall with my shouts of relief and happiness, which included letting go of the steering wheel to do a little dance, hence the almost crashing into the wall.

I ran down to the excavation site and told Fernando the good news. He told me that the cart had still been there when he had passed early. We both ran to the museum and called Jose before the *payés* could change his mind.

Jose arrived twenty minutes later. I saw a mischievous look in Fernando's eye and I yelled, "Don't even think about it!"

"It would only take an hour or so to finish the road."

"Fernando, I am warning you, if you use that bridge one more time, I am going to go and personally ask the *payés* to bring the cart back."

Jose helped by adding, "And I don't want any more problems with the *payés*."

Fernando muttered, "Fine."

Jose went to collect his tractor.

The archaeology students walk to the site. We leave the large inexpensive tools on site, under a tarp. The expensive tools and archaeological finds are brought back each day by the students and staff. It works perfectly.

The plan sounds vaguely familiar.

15

Letters from Home

I never notice how much I change until I go back home. It is like my hair; I see it every day and it looks the same even though, little by little, it grows, and, instead of noticing a difference, I adjust to it as if that is the way it had always been. For me, this is the hardest part about living in a different country... these small changes that make me feel I belong nowhere. I will never feel Spanish, yet, after five years abroad, I don't feel I fit into the States anymore either. I so envy people who feel they are from a certain place... who know where home is and where they will end up.

When I studied in Mexico, I made many friends and, while they all had their very separate personality and identities, they all had a common bond of being and feeling Mexican. Their conviction and pride of being of Mexican heritage caused me to feel like a perpetual, jealous outsider. I often wonder, what is my culture? Where is my home? I am not sure that I will ever have answers to those questions, but letters from home, even if they can't make me feel like I still belong there, remind me without a doubt where I am from and the place that made me who I am.

Letters from my mom remind me of our special and easy relationship. Of sitting outside at night listening to the frogs and toads croaking in the creek. Of her humor that is also my humor, which borders on demented. Of barbecued steak and home-grown vegetables. Tomatoes so thick and ripe and good that I ate them raw like apples. Of unconditional and guiltless love that not only allows, but encourages my adventures around the world.

Letters from my brother make me laugh and remind me that life is not so complicated; one can relax and it does not mean the end of the world. His bad luck that he takes with such humor, whether it be getting sick again or being robbed in Mexico or having his airline fold up before his return flight, leaving him stranded and penniless, reminds me of how lucky I am and how I should not take my luck for granted... especially since he thinks I wound up with both of our luck.

Letters from my sister, Roni, show me that you do not need to entirely understand someone to love them. We are opposites in every way. Her letters are usually an inventory of what is in the package she sent; however, the packages are usually more thoughtful and caring than any words could be and are her way of sending me a little bit of home.

Emails from Carisa remind me what it is to have a best friend and to be one. I don't think we ever make friends like we do when we are adolescent... when your best friend *is* your life and you wear necklaces with the words 'best friend' cut in half, each wearing one side to announce your friendship to others. Carisa reminds me of mischief and fun and the feeling of immortality that only belongs to the very young.

My Aunt Anne's letters remind me of where I come from, traditions and of the land I grew up on. Her letters are full of description of the landscape and how it changes with the seasons, life on the ranch and day-to-day occurrences that make me feel like I am not an ocean away. Her letters always fill me with nostalgia and remind me that I am a person with roots... who came from somewhere. That I do have history. She is the keeper of the family tree and reminds me of the adventures that my ancestors had and that I am now adding to by leaving my hometown after four generations. My aunt's letters remind me to look for beauty in simple things, long walks, stones, belly flowers (because they are so small you have to get on your belly to see them), a hard day's work, and taking what comes at you and making the best of it.

Letters from home help me to feel centered here. It is so easy to lose my sense of balance being surrounded by so many reminders that scream at me that I am not from here. Letters from loved ones help to remind me that I am me no matter where I am.

Lana,

Its Memorial Day weekend and it's raining and the wind is blowing. Boat drags have been canceled. I on the other hand have a great book to read; the creek has held extraordinary life since I have fenced it off, making for great walks with the dogs. I now have deer, quail and even wild turkeys.

Splurged on the good wine and there is a race on TV later. Tell me, does life get any better? Oh yes, I forgot to mention that I only have seven working days left till my three-month vacation this year. Better believe I am a happy camper. Lane said he talked to you; that always makes me happy that you are able to stay in touch. How is the good life there on the island? I am sad that I am not going this year. But hopefully I can get a lot done here and maintain a weight loss program where I actually lose weight. Read you tomorrow (AKA talk to you tomorrow on email). I know, sometimes my cleverness amazes me too.

Love you lots.
Mom

Lana,

Que pasa? How is everything going there w/ your school/life? Hope the gas/diesel crunch isn't hurting you guys too much. I know it must be expensive w/ Fernando driving the bus to Ciutadella and the museo every day. I heard about the strikes that have been going on there w/ the fishermen and truckers. How bad is it on the island? Out here, the gas is outrageous! $4.50/gal. I know that is about half of what it is out there. My truck is an 8 cylinder that gets about 8 miles to the gallon. Good thing I never have to drive too far.

So today I am not working. Yesterday was demolition day, where I have to wear a respirator and jacket because of all the insulation and metal scraps. Real shitty job in the humidity and it takes about 10 hrs. Well about an hour into it, it felt like I was breathing fire into my respirator; I was freezing w/ goose bumps everywhere. So I took a bath at lunch because I couldn't eat (my throat was fucked; couldn't barely swallow). Worked the rest of the day then went to the doctor. I had a 103.2 degree temp. + strep throat. So I am sitting here trying to figure out how to drink this damn mate. Do you know? I have the mate straw, and the mate but no gourd. I put some in a glass, poured cold water over it, then hot water, but all the stuff floats. Is that right? Oh well.

Hope all is well out there. Hit me back w/ some stories, hot students, etc...

Tell Fernando I said hola.
Lane

Hola,

How is everyone there? Is Paula there yet? Tell her I said hi. I don't know if the world stations are picking up the California fires or not but boy it is pretty bad. We had a summer storm the other day, I was telling you about it when I called. I went to Chico later that day to watch a baseball game and I kept seeing these lightning strikes. They would come from the sky straight down and hit the ground. This was during the day and you could see it. It didn't branch out like most lightning bolts do. Well the next morning we started hearing how many fires we had. There are over a 1000 (yes thousand) fires going in the state. There are 130 in Shasta county, 30 in Tehama county and 78 in Butte county. There are not enough firefighters to help. They are working horrendous shifts and there are no backups coming. We had just gotten a fire in Paradise under control a few days before this storm. There were 70 homes lost and 1000 people in shelters. That was when the wind was so bad they couldn't stop the fire at all even with lots of firefighters from other places coming in to help. Now it's pretty bleak. Platina (my favorite place to ride my motorcycle) is being evacuated and there is only one truck on its way to try to fight it. The wind has totally stopped so the smoke has settled into the valley here and the air quality has reached very unhealthy levels. There is only one level left and that is hazardous. A normal air quality day is 10. Today it is 205. Needless to say you need to stay indoors and not do anything strenuous. As far as any fires right here in Red Bluff, there are not any. We are supposed to get more thunder storms on Friday. Wow! How things change quickly. I was going to do some hiking but not now. Two hikers got lost on Shasta and when they were found 2 days later they said that the smoke got so bad that they got disoriented. Hopefully some other states will be able to send firefighters; otherwise, we are in for the long haul. Any how I'm sure if you check the news you will hear about us. Of course the rains back east are so bad that is on national news also. All along the Mississippi River the deltas are breaking from all of the water and entire towns are being flooded. It is crazy around here. Life right here is actually good. The air is really bad but at least we are safe for the time being. Thinking of you guys in Spain!

Love
Mom

Lana,

Thank you for always being you and never trying to be someone else. I love the you, you are. Besides wishing you the very best of birthdays, I wanted to say thank you. Thank you for being the best thing that ever happened to me and giving me the happiest memories that I can ever imagine. When I'm feeling melancholy I think of the things we've been through, whether together or separated by oceans, I have felt the joy and pain with you. And when I laugh I feel I'm sharing all those impossibly wonderful times and things we have done. This past trip to Spain was a once in a lifetime experience and you have been a part of many of those, but this felt like a more special time this time. I needed that time with you. And hurray! It was grand. So be sure to tell Fernando I appreciated his thoughtfulness beyond words. In either language.

I hope that your time off was revitalizing. And are looking forward to starting the season.

Hugs and kisses.
Be well and safe.
Love you <u>always</u>
Mom

My sister, Roni, does not write long, descriptive letters, but sends me her love in her way and makes me remember home.

After recently being married, a package arrived at my new address in Spain. When I opened it, I was surprised to see a blue, three-ringed binder. When I opened it, I could not help but laugh and be extremely grateful. It was a cookbook for dummies. My sister tactfully did not put it that way, but as I read over the different recipes that she had written out by hand (making it so much more special) I realized that she must have looked over all of her cookbooks and copied down the easiest to prepare while at the same time keeping in mind my likes and what I would and would not be able to purchase on an island. I am the only family member who cannot cook and I am sure that my sister was worried how this would affect my marriage to a Spaniard. My sister is very much of the opinion that 'a way to a man's heart is through his stomach'. Lucky for me, there are other ways.

Another package from my sister was very light. When I opened it, again I could not stifle my laughter. There were a few packets of beautiful glass beads (I had recently told her that I had taken up silver smithing as a hobby and often used stone and glass beads), but the majority of the space was taken up with OB tampons, regular. I could have kissed her. On the island, I can find my favorite, environmentally conscience, made by a woman tampons; however, 'regular' in Spain seems not to be quite the same. I am not sure if there is a difference in menstruation between the Mediterranean and the USA, but the tampons imply there is. I bought a box of regular OB tampons here on the island and brought the unopened box with me to work. The time came when it was necessary to open the box. When I saw the size, I paled and I checked the label. 'Regular'. Regular my ass. With some deep breathing and yoga, I was able to finish the task. My mother must have told my sister this story and my truly wonderful, even if very different from me, sister took action.

> *Lana,*
>
> *I miss you so much lately, it is so weird. Things that you have taught me throughout my life have been popping into my head lately. Like how you would always get mad at me for being mean to my mom. I apologized to her for that the other night and she cried. Or the time when I found that spider on the wall and I wanted to kill it and you caught it instead and put it outside. You have always been like that and it seems like every day lately some memory like that pops into my mind. The universe is trying to tell me something. You are so precious and I am still learning from you and knowing that just makes me miss you so much more.*
>
> *Can't wait till we talk again,*
> *Carisa*

Queridos:

Here I am in a conference in Redding with Ellen. This conference is for people with disabilities. It is called People First. They use the name People First because they want to be seen as a person first, not as a disability.

Lana, I have to tell you how much pleasure the cookie for my birthday gave me. A cookie from Rio Limay in Argentina!! I'm afraid that I could lose it with the other cookies under the tree; therefore, the cookie is on our front porch with some little Indian rocks. A place of more importance for this cookie!![14]

For my birthday, we took a drive to the wildlife area near Willows. It was a rainy day, but we had an amazing drive around the levees, looking at the ducks and water fowl. Then we went to Chico to the Olive Garden for dinner. On John's birthday we

---

[14]When my brother and I were little, my aunt often took us for long walks along the creek. She was obsessed with finding perfectly flat and round rocks, which she called cookies. She would take the best cookies of the day home and place them around a tree in her yard, which we named the cookie tree. Lane and I loved to elicit cries from her by finding perfect cookies and say, 'what a great skipping rock' as we cocked our arms back pretending we were going to skip it on the surface of the creek's water. Many years later when I was having a rare homesick day, in need of a bond to home, I decided to start sending my aunt international cookies, linking the country that I was currently in to traditions, past and home.

drove the back way to Paskenta. We tried to dive up to the Eagle Peak Lookout to have a picnic but ran into snow! I hope your birthday was wonderful. I'm sure that Fernando did something very special for you.

This spring has been beautiful. The flowers have been exceptional. It started with the plum tree covered with tiny white blooms, just like a big snowball, then the quince with its salmon blossoms. The wild brodea's bluish-purple blooms were absolutely everywhere. I can never remember them being so prolific. Fields were just covered with the blooms. Next came the Oregon grape in a profusion of yellow blossoms and yellow bees and after that the lilacs and the red bud. The old-fashioned yellow rose is blooming now and it is beautiful. There must have been some sort of phenomena in the weather that made it a good year for blossoms. I can't remember a year when there were so many beautiful flowers.

The Red Bluff Round Up has come and gone. Ellen had another of her magical times. She had hugs from Bob Tallman, the rodeo announcer who announces the National Finals Rodeo, got her picture taken with Lloyd Ferguson, the driver of the Budweiser Clydesdales hitch, met Wayne Brooks, the other rodeo announcer and most important, spent significant time with John

Payne, the one-armed bandit who is the rodeo specialty act. He is her hero. She also won the drawing for the belt buckle given by Dodge Trucks. What a weekend! We did have a bad incident when a bucking bull jumped into the stands and injured some people. From our vantage point, it looked like a bunch of people had gathered around a fight, then I saw the back of the gray bull. Of course, the rodeo board is concerned about a possible law suit and all are saying very little.

This has been a very dry spring, sounds like one of the driest on record. The reservoirs on the ranch did not fill last year or this year. Hopefully, they won't go dry. Just 20 miles to the north, at the other ranch on Cottonwood Creek, the reservoirs all filled. Can you believe that there is that much difference in weather between the two ranches? The hills started turning brown by the middle of April. It is drying out at least a month earlier than usual.

John is getting ready to cut our oat crop for hay. Hopefully it will make good hay. The price of hay has gone up drastically and we will have to buy some to get through the summer, but hopefully our hay will offset some of the need. We plan to sell the calves and cull some of the older cows due to the drought. With the high hay prices, it is hard to justify feeding the whole herd through the summer. I haven't started the vegetable garden yet. Just as well, because there was a freeze on April 20 that wiped out a lot of other gardeners' tomato plants and other vegetable plants.

John has been busy cutting wood. I hope his sore back holds together. Numerous trees went down during the January 4 storm and there have been two other wind storms that have knocked down more trees. We know a couple of men who are in need of work, so John is dealing with them to cut some of the downed trees and give them a share of the wood...

A huge bottom oak blew down in the west Johnson flat and the wood cutters were cutting it up. They had stacked the brush, so John decided before it got too dry that he should burn up the brush. He lit the fires and when they burned down pretty well, he came home for dinner. After dinner he went to check on his fires. Shortly, he came rushing down the hill in the old brown truck and I knew something was wrong. The fires had crept into the sawdust and had crawled into the rounds of wood that were stacked there. Greg, Ted and I hurried to help. We worked with water, ax, shovel and tractor to keep the fire from spreading. The wind started to blow and John was forced to cover with dirt the stump that was full of live cinders. Just a normal evening at the Read Ranch!

The house at the Dry Creek Ranch is an old school house that Sam brought there in the 1930s. Due to old age, lack of care and bad foundation, the building is sinking into the ground and falling apart. We are in the process of deciding what to do. We took Brooke Kinner out there and he says that the house is not fixable for human habitation. Now, what to do? We can get a mobile home, or we can get a kit house and have Brooke build it. Our renter needs a shop for his taxidermy work. Should we fix up the old house for a shop or should we build a new garage for him to use? Decisions, decisions.

Speaking of old buildings, the new Cone Kimball clock tower was dedicated last weekend. It was really a fun gathering with lots of 'old Red Bluff' in attendance. At the stroke of noon, the final piece of the tower was attached and it was Brooke who climbed up the fire engine ladder to put the weather vane in place. It was extra special for us to know the fellow who got that honor.

I went to a Down Syndrome conference in Chico two weeks ago. It was awesome. It validated a lot of things that I had intuitively known for many years. I guess the most important thing was that self-talk goes with the syndrome. For many years I have been trying to correct and teach Ellen not to talk to herself, now I know it is 'normal' for her. It has been a problem at the work place and she has been criticized for it. Now I can tell the critics to bug off!!

Meanwhile, back at the Redding conference, right now we are sitting waiting for dinner. Chris Burke of Life Goes On *is going to perform with his band. Are you old enough to remember Corky with Down Syndrome from the TV show* Life Goes On? *It was an awesome show and we were so sad when it went off the air. We are watching them set up for the show. Ellen adores Chris Burke and is very taken with him. Maybe if we are lucky she will get to talk with him or dance with or even eat dinner with him. Maybe... then again, maybe he will ignore her because she has tried maybe too hard to get his attention. More latter.*

NEXT CHAPTER: I'm now home and have got to fill you in on the evening! Earlier in the day I had visited with the twin brothers who make up the rest of Chris Burk's band. They were instructors at a music camp and this is how they met Chris. So, Ellen and I were watching the band set up and when they finished, the brothers (Joe and John) came over and asked if they could sit with us. That was pretty cool. Then Chris showed up and Joe told him to sit by Ellen. So he did. WHEEEE!! Ellen's first words to him were, "I have a boyfriend." I was ready to kill her, but Chris replied, "I have a girlfriend and her name is Annie." That seemed to clear the air between them and the rest of the evening went great. He's a bit impressed with this star status, but very nice and also very much a person with Down Syndrome. Earlier in the day I saw him in the dining room having an animated conversation with himself, complete with hand gestures. Just a little Down Syndrome self-talk!

I guess I had better close. I would love to have you explain to me about your three excavation projects. You say you were excavating the Roman military fort and now will be working on the Roman City of Sanisera and the Necropolis? You'll have to tell me about the projects some day. It would be great if we could actually talk to each other on the phone, but it seems like I am not destined to be home when you call. I keep thinking about the internet.... Still just thinking, no action yet. Don't hold your breath.

Love you both,
Aunty Anne.

Honestly, I do not know what I have done to deserve such wonderful, understanding and caring people in my life. Thank you. Your love and understanding keep me on track of the Lana I want to be.

16

Adaptation Secret

Mary, a single British woman who I often chat with, told me she was considering moving here after her quickly approaching retirement, but was worried that she would not be able to adjust to island life on a daily basis. She had bought her second home in Es Migjorn Gran when the currency was still *pesetas*. She was struggling with her decision because she could now sell her house on Menorca for five times what she bought it for, or she could become one of the many ex-pats on the island. She was worried that Menorca would not be the same when actually living here as it was while vacationing here. She had her doubts as to whether she could acclimatize to year-round Menorca. She wanted to know my secret, my 'adaptation secret', as she called it. I tried to tell her, but realized as I stuttered to make a complete and coherent sentence that I did not know myself.

All that night, I thought about it. What was it that made me not freak out at all of the changes in my life? Was it my patient, kind and furry Spanish husband, Fernando? Was it my ever-supportive family who adores Fernando and maybe more importantly adore the idea that they have a free place to stay in a Mediterranean paradise? Am I just a rootless person who can settle anywhere? What was it that made me feel at home here? What was it that helped me to establish my identity in this foreign place?

As often happens when I put a questions to my brain at night, I get the delayed answer sometime during the next morning when I have completely forgotten about whatever it was that I was asking myself. The next day as I was slowing to a stop in front of the first of three cattle guards I pass on my way to work, it hit me... animals. My secret to adapting so easily to this entirely new and different life and establishing an identity here was all the litter critters that I spend so much time with and take care of.

Animals have always played an important role in who I am. When I was little, I dreamed of being a veterinarian until I started to realize that all people don't treat their animals the way my family does. If I would have become a veterinarian, I most likely would have been fired my first week for refusing to give animals back to unworthy owners. After I accepted that I could not pursue my childhood dream job, I did a job shadow with our local fish and game warden. The job seemed very gratifying, but the temptation to shoot evil poachers was just too great for me. I decided that my desire to help and protect animals would have to be a part of my life outside of work. It was apparent that it was too difficult for me to be professional with something that affected me so personally. But without a doubt, one way or another, I have always known that animals have to be in my life.

The first time that I visited Menorca, I was pleasantly surprised at how rural the island was. Large expansions of farm land dotted by little white towns topped with red tile roofs. Fernando knew that I liked spending time in nature from his visit to California and planned accordingly. On our hikes along the coast, we found turtles in the wildflowers, saw rabbits darting about, and were awed by the abundance of different migrating birds that graced us with their brief presence after their long flight from Africa.

I was in nature heaven.

When I began to work in the museum, I thought I caught glimpses of fur in the wood pile next to the stone wall in the forest. I asked Fernando about it.

"Yeah, there are tons of stray cats that live around this farmhouse. They eat the rats. You will always find stray cats around large farmhouses that don't have dogs. People dump them out there to get rid of them. The farmers usually let them be if they eat the rats and stay out of sight."

I decided that I was going to tame the cats in my spare time. I started by leaving food out by the wood pile always singing the same 'here kitty' song each time so they would get used to me and associate me with food. After about a week, two cats started coming out while I set the food down; a striped gray one that I named Rey and a black one that I named Sheeba. After another week, they would eat while I sat near murmuring to them. By the end of the month, I could pet them while they ate. There were many more cats in the wood pile, but I focused my attentions on these two. There was a huge orange cat that Fernando said he had seen from the beginning that I also tried at first with, but he did not seem the least bit interested in making friends and I decided that it was probably too late to change his ways. Whereas Sheeba and Rey were still quite small and longing for attention. Midway through the season, they started following me back to the museum, only dashing to the wood pile if loud customers came.

During the afternoon lull in customers, they would come and lounge with me. One day, I saw Sheeba at Rey's neck poking around. I had no idea what she was doing until I saw her drop a tick on the ground. She continued de-ticking Rey for another five minutes. I could not believe it. I knew that monkeys did these kinds of things, but had no

idea that cats did. Rey, the bitch, did not return the favor
and Sheeba won a very special place in my heart that day.

Now that they were my pets, I decided the correct thing
to do would be to have them spayed because we were in a
natural reserve and I did not want a bunch of kittens eating
all of the geckos and turtledoves that frequented the patio. I
asked Fernando how much it would cost and he said over
100€ each because they were female. 100€! I thought that
Fernando was mistaken because that was just a ridiculously
high price that could not possibly be right. I called a local
vet. 115€ per female! Ridiculous. Absolutely ridiculous,
especially considering the cat infestation problem on
Menorca.

Because there were so many feral cats on the island, I
was sure there had to be some program that neutered feral
cats for free on certain days. I called everywhere, vet
offices, city hall, environmental organizations and nothing.
There was no prevention plan on the island. The only plan
to control the cat problem was extermination. I was even
asked to give the location of the cat infestation that I was
calling about so that they could exterminate them. I
slammed the phone down and hoped it hurt the listener's
ear.

I wanted to do the responsible thing, but that was not as
easy as I had thought it would be. I did not have 230€ to
spare. I was recently out of college and recently married
and did not have the extra money.

As if to mock my efforts and frustration, a white demon
cat showed up a few days later and started 'come have sex
with me' meows from somewhere in the forest. Sheeba and
Rey hated him and beseeched me to protect their virtue. I
threw rocks while they growled.

My brother, Lane, was staying with me when the
demon cat showed up. He agreed that the cat did, indeed, to
appear to be evil. It was all white with pink skin that seeped

through his fur. He had green eyes that were evil. There is no other way to explain those eyes... pure evil. Paula (her first year at the museum), animal lover that she is, concurred with our evil cat opinion.

My brother, just to spite us now seeing that Paula and I were in agreement, said, "Poor cat. He can't help his horrible appearance. I am sure that the people who dumped him out here neglected and abused him. And he calls every evening not for the female cats, but out of his need for love and attention. And what does he get for these sincere attempts? Rocks. Poor, poor cat."

We both knew that Lane was being a shit, but were both affected by this new concept of the demon cat. Later that evening, I took a bit of food out to where he was calling. He scrunched down when I placed the food in front of him as if waiting to be hit. I was overwhelmed with guilt when I thought of the rocks I had thrown after him before. He let me pet him and I changed his name from Demon Cat to Felipe. From that day on, he became the most popular figure of the weird animal zoo that would later come to be in the Ecomuseum.

A few weeks later, it was obvious that Sheeba was pregnant.

While Sheeba got fatter and fatter, I started to keep a list of all of the cats I had seen from time to time. Twenty-four cats. This was out of control. Twenty-four cats plus what Sheeba was going to have within the next few days.

Felipe soon showed us that he had no shame. As soon as a customer would sit down to relax and enjoy their drink and the view, Felipe would pounce onto the lap of this un-expecting person. When people tried shoo him off, he would anchor on with his nails and the only way to disengage him was by ripping clothing. While organizing products in the museum's store, I heard a startled, "Oh my."

Felipe had jumped onto the lap of an elderly British tourist who was enjoying her coffee with milk. She was a repeat customer and I was determined to get Felipe off her without damaging her clothing. When I apologized, she sincerely said, "No, no, I love cats; he just startled me; that's all."

I began to tell her the cat problems we were having and she asked in a disbelieving tone, "You don't know Janice?" I told her I did not.

"Janice is a wonderful woman. She is English, but has spent much of her life on the island and dedicates all of her free time to helping cats. She has a self-made, self-run organization. She opens up her home on Sundays and sells baked goods, cat Christmas cards and similar items. All of this money goes towards helping and neutering feral cats on the island. She has neutered over four thousand feral cats on Menorca."

Shit, why had I not heard of her before? I was given her number and called her that evening. She said she would be out before the week was over. She made good on her promise. I was expecting a nice, pleasant woman, and was surprised by the jaded woman who I greeted. She had some cat food and two cages that slammed shut when a long string was pulled. She told me she worked best alone. I left her at it and closed up the museum.

She asked me what I expected her to do with the neutered cats, and I said she could bring them back. I would feed them so that they would not attack so readily the natural fauna. With this, she softened and, after a few stories, I understood her bitterness. People only called Janice when they wanted a cat problem fixed, but did not want to feel responsible for the deaths of all the creatures. Most who called her did not give donations or support her cause in any way. She had received many calls from people saying, 'if you don't come and get these kittens, I am going to put them in a bag and throw them in the sea'. Her resentment was more than understandable and I remembered again why I like animals more than people.

She only caught half of the feral cats that night. We agreed that once the trapped cats were neutered, she would drop them off and come back for the rest. During this time, Sheeba had her kittens. This black cat produced four pure white babies (thank you, Demon Cat) and one smoke-colored one. They were all beautiful. When Janice arrived, I led her to where I had found Sheeba with her babies. Janice looked lovingly at them and then cursed. I was surprised. She explained that, because of the intense light in Menorca, all white cats had skin cancer and eventually died from it. This is why Felipe looked so pink. Cancer. Janice told me that she did not snip the left ear of white cats as she did with all other cats she neutered, marking them so that she would not re-catch them in the future, because scars, being hairless, were more vulnerable to cancer. She went about trapping the rest of the cats. We lowered Felipe and Rey into cages as well.

When she dropped off the rest of the cats, she told me her veterinary friend from Germany was on her way back home and had offered to take Sheeba and all of her babies to her farm where they would have an abandoned stable all to themselves. I had such mixed emotions. I wanted what was best for Sheeba's new babies and knew that was the less intensely lighted Germany, but it broke my heart. What if Sheeba did not like it, tried to run away and got lost? Finally, I agreed, and today I still receive happy reports of my now-German cat and her babies.

Janice told me that she had found a vet on the island who would do all neutering of cats half price for her. This was still a fortune and I offered to pay, little by little, the cost of the cats from Cavalleria. I also donated silver jewelry, which was my new hobby, for her to sell in her house on Sundays. I am happy to say this became a tradition.

A while later, Janice emailed me. She wrote a column in an English magazine and wanted Felipe to be cat of the month. I sent a few pictures of the evil cat and he was famous for all of May. Readers of the magazine brought him special treats, which helped him on his mission of becoming the fattest cat in the world.

Once, while Felipe was stretched out on the floor, a British tourist walked up to him and lovingly stroked his fat belly. She smiled to herself and lovingly murmured to Felipe, "Kittens, oh kittens."

"He's male, just very fat."

She jerked her hand back as if she had been stung, and said, "GROSS!"

That was a pretty accurate description. Felipe was so fat by this time that he could not even properly clean himself, and Paula, the saint that she is, would sometimes swipe his behind with a warm cloth to do the job that he could not.

One afternoon, the huge orange cat that I had never previously seen during midday waltzed over and started drinking from the stone sink that later became known as 'Gary the seagull's sink', and started to drink delicately. I called him and he let out the squeakiest, high-pitched meow that I have heard uttered from a cat's lips. Definitely not what I had been expecting from such a large cat. I called again and he came over and wanted to be petted. I had tried unsuccessfully for almost a year to tame him and now he just walked over? But that was how it was with Manolo. From that day on, he has never missed a day at the museum.

*   *   *   *

"Do you speak English?" a pair of concerned-looking British tourists asked me when they walked into the museum.

Their backpacks, shoes and sweat told me that they had been walking and I dreaded to hear what they looked so concerned about. After I told them I spoke English, they said something that would start a personal mission for me.

"We just came walking from the beach of Cavalleria. You know there is a cattle guard there, right?"

I think they were subtly trying to find out if I knew what a cattle guard was. It is amazing the amount of people who do not, but, in all fairness, why would someone from the city know that livestock won't cross rails with a hole under it? I always worry that an animal will try when under stress, for example a car spooking it, and break its legs between the rails. But I have never seen or heard of this happening. I assured the tourists that I knew the cattle guard they were speaking of and was worried that, indeed, my fear had come true.

"There is a frightened hedgehog trapped in it. It is curled up in a ball, but still alive."

Paula and I exchanged looks of 'how and the hell could we have been so dense as to not have thought of that before'. There were not many customers and I told Paula to 'go; go; go'. She grabbed a cloth to protect her hands and was out of there.

She was back in about ten minutes with a very hot little hedgehog. We brought him into the kitchen where it was cooler and shut off the lights. We set a plate of water next to him and, when he felt safe enough, he un-balled, sniffed the water and then started lapping at it with a thick, little pink tongue. After he refreshed himself, Paula took him to the field and left him in the shade under a bush. From then on, we stopped every morning on the way to work at each of the three cattle guards that we crossed daily.

The cattle guards are ridiculously and unnecessarily deep. Lying flat on our stomachs (on the road used by fast-driving tourists), we could still not reach the bottom. We started with a board and one would shimmy the trapped hedgehog up the corner (obligingly, the little creatures stayed in a ball, making it much easier) while the other reached down and grabbed the little animal with gloved hands and freed it from the rails. We would then place it on the other side of the nearest stone wall so that it could not easily wander back into the trap.

This was fine until I started staying later at work as the tourist season picked up, consequently arriving later to work. Our current saving technique was a two-man operation and we were no longer traveling together. I was trying to figure out what to do while filling up for gas before going to work. The gas station that I use is in the center of the island and has all types of tourist paraphernalia imaginable. Postcards, snorkel and mask set, air cushions, etc. It was the small fishing net that kids use on the beach that caught my attention. It had a strong yet flexible wire rim and a sturdy net. It was connected to a long blue pole.

I checked the cattle guards, but there were no babies to save that day. I walked into the museum proudly carrying my net. Paula, one of the wittiest people I have ever met, had no doubt as to what it was for.

"That is one nice HRD you've got there."

"What?" I asked, slow on the uptake.

"Sorry, that is one nice Hedgehog Rescuing Device you have there."

I smiled at the acronym, but was troubled that Paula, an English as a second language speaker, was cleverer in my language than I was.

This tool greatly eased our rescues. We could individually save hedgehogs quickly and efficiently, greatly reducing our risk of being run over.

The first year, we did not keep track of how many hedgehogs we saved, but it was a lot. The next year, we started counting. The summer of 2007 yielded thirty-seven hedgehogs, the main months being July and August. In 2008, twenty-nine hedgehogs and one turtle were pulled by us from their certain death, concentrating again in July and August.

Paula and I thought, because Menorca is a biosphere reserve, some organization would do something about this once it was brought to their attention, and not leave the task of saving this at risk indigenous creature to two foreign girls. We called everyone... City hall, the equivalent of fish and game and environmental organizations (I will not specify because there are various and because it makes me too angry to do so, especially because one of them sells a children's book that all the schools buy as well as tourists for 10€ a pop about how this organization helps an injured baby hedgehog). Everyone gave me the appropriate horrified response and the run around.

I have been nagging for four years now. Are ramps that hard to build? I wrote to the main newspaper in Menorca and they took me seriously enough to rewrite my Spanish article in Menorquín and print the photos that I sent them of scared hedgehogs being pulled out of the cattle guards. Another local paper later wrote a full-page article with photos and called me 'the hedgehog saving woman of the island'. Even the news station for the three islands IB3 did an interview with me pulling hedgehogs out of cattle guards with my HRD. But still no preventative measures have taken place.

I still have hopes that something will be done. Until then, I continue to pull them out and inform anyone who will listen. I am now also known as the crazy Yankee who saves hedgehogs. Hey, at least I have made my niche.

*   *   *   *

The scene started off the same way the discovery of the hedgehogs did, except that the couple was German. With their broken English, they communicated to us that a baby goat had fallen about three meters down the cliff side by the lighthouse and was stuck on a small ledge.

I told them that we would take care of it, not at all confident in my words. Paula and I both agreed that we would leave it for the night because goats had an amazing way of navigating mountain and cliff sides and maybe it was not trapped at all.

The next morning proved differently. It was still there and noticeably weaker. First, we called the farmer whose goats they were. He did not seem to overly care. To his defense, he had a very full day of ranch work without having to save baby goats. I was happy enough that he fed and watered them, which many farmers on the island do not do with goats. I was also happy that he did not hobble them by placing a huge weight around their necks, or by tying two goats together, or by tying on one side the front and back legs of a goat together. These were all tactics that I had seen other farmers on the island use when trying to control escaping goats.

The *payés* of Cavalleria goats escaped plenty, but he does not blame the goats. He rightfully blames the tourists. On the way to the lighthouse, there is a gate that says in seven different languages 'please close the gate'. In English, it actually says, 'please close the door', but it is easy enough to understand. However, people constantly leave it open. At night, after a long day of work and after the herd of sunset watchers have left, I often walked the five minutes to the gate, close it and walk back before going home. The farmer waits until around mid-September when tourism declines noticeably and rounds up all the loose goats in the area. He never punishes the goats, and, therefore, I could forgive him if he did not want to save one goat by dangling out on a dangerous cliff ledge.

We then called the fire department. I had been hoping for the kind of fire department that saves frighten kittens from high tree limbs. No. They told me their job was to put out fires. Period. The local police said it was not something they could help with, but wished us the best of luck. The environmental organization on the islands said they only help indigenous fauna of the island.

"And the hedgehogs of Cavalleria that I call you about every month?"

Pause… "Yeah, we're… ah… working on that."

"Man, you guys are thorough. Years now and you're still working on the amazing escape route for the hedgehogs that fall in the cattle guards. How much money did you guys make this year off your book that tells children your organization helps baby hedgehogs?" I asked before I hung up.

Saving the baby goat now fell on the shoulders of Paula and Lana. I held the fort down while Paula went upstairs and rummaged through the museum's storage, which held a plethora of seemingly useless items, a few archaeological excavation tools and some agricultural supplies. She came down with a long, narrow tube of PVC piping and a very long rope. I saw exactly what she was up to. All we had to do was fold the rope in half and push U-shaped part down the pipe. When the rope came out the other end, it looked like a noose. All we had to do was slip the loose rope over the baby's neck, pull the ends of the rope that came out the other end of the PVC pipe and drag the baby goat up the cliff before we strangled it.

When Paula showed me an example, I said, "That is one nice GRD."

It was her turn to be slow on the uptake and I explained, "Goat Rescuing Device."

We closed up before sunset and followed the procession of tourists up to the lighthouse. No one watched the sunset that night.

People looked at us strangely as we walked towards the cliff edge with a PVC pipe and a long black rope. After talking it over, it seemed that Paula had more experience with roping animals than I did, so she was going to put the noose around the goat's small neck. We had to be quick about it because we feared that, if we scared the goat before we had it secure, it might fall to its death, ninety meters below.

We practiced a few times with a log, the crowd around us ever growing. People seemed to understand the need for silence and watched in bemusement as we established our plan. Paula was going to dangle half of her body over the cliff's edge. I was to hold onto one of her legs with one hand and the ends of the rope from the PVC pipe in the other. I was going to be sitting so that, if she slid towards the cliff's edge by the weight of the struggling goat, I could counterbalance. Also, I had to pull the end of the rope, tightening the noose when Paula yelled 'okay', securing the baby goat. Once it was secure with the noose tight around its neck, Paula was going to fall back using her weight and momentum to pull the goat up while I scooted backwards at the same speed so as to keep the noose tight.

We took our positions just as the sun was setting. Everyone was facing north with us and the cliff face. Today in Cavalleria, only the dead Romans head's faced towards the west.

I imagined the headlines tomorrow. 'Argentinean girl killed trying to save baby goat while stupid North American looks on'.

I tried to chase the image of Paula plummeting to her death from my mind and concentrate on the plan. She dangled while I held her leg in my hand. She yelled, 'okay', and I pulled the ends of the rope, tightening the noose. She fell back and I scooted back. The baby goat did not need to be forcefully hauled up. He helped us by scaling the cliff side as we pulled. In seconds, it was over. The baby goat was next to us. We loosened the noose and set it free while people cheered around us. We congratulated each other, basking in our success. As the cheers faded, we heard the baby goat crying out as it ran towards Cala Viola. Within seconds, its cries were answered by a deeper cry coming from 'goat beach'. Animals are so much less complicated. No explanation was necessary. The baby goat went straight for his mother's udder and she let her baby fill himself while she stood and chewed her cud.

*   *   *   *

I never experienced the culture shock that many people talk about when arriving in a new country. Yes many things surprised me and continue to surprise me. I am constantly learning about this country and its people and will do so until I die... hopefully in the distant future and here on Menorca. I plan on joining the trend in Menorca of living past one hundred.

I am sure if I had moved to Madrid or Barcelona, I would have been impacted by culture shock and gone running back to the USA. I need nature. I need to see beauty. I need to feel safe. I need to be surrounded by good people. All of these things helped me to adjust to my new way of life in Menorca, but it was my love and adventures with little island creatures that have helped me the most. They listen to all of my stories and aren't bothered by the masculine and feminine errors I make when speaking this difficult language. They don't get confused when I conjugate a verb incorrectly, or use the wrong tense. They are not offended if I use the more familiar *tú* instead of *usted* when addressing them. They have helped me, and continue to help me, to establish my identity in a foreign land. They help me to feel more like me. They are my 'adaptation secret'.

* * * *

A local told me when talking about foreigners (meaning anyone not born on the island), "Menorca either accepts you or rejects you and you know which fate has befallen you right away."

I know that I will never be a local, no matter how hard I try to 'go native', but I would like to thank Menorca for welcoming me. I feel, in all my weirdness, accepted here.

CPSIA information can be obtained at www.ICGtesting.com
Printed in the USA
BVOW07s0018081013

333092BV00014BA/351/P